LIBRARY HISTORY

LIBRARY HISTORY

AN EXAMINATION GUIDEBOOK

SECOND EDITION FULLY REVISED AND ENLARGED

BY JAMES G OLLÉ FLA

Gordon Herbert

SENIOR LECTURER, SCHOOL OF LIBRARIANSHIP
LOUGHBOROUGH TECHNICAL COLLEGE

ARCHON BOOKS & CLIVE BINGLEY

FIRST PUBLISHED 1967

SECOND EDITION FULLY REVISED AND ENLARGED
FIRST PUBLISHED 1971 BY CLIVE BINGLEY LTD
THIS EDITION SIMULTANEOUSLY PUBLISHED IN THE USA
BY ARCHON BOOKS, THE SHOE STRING PRESS INC,
995 SHERMAN AVENUE, HAMDEN,
CONNECTICUT 06514
PRINTED IN GREAT BRITAIN
COPYRIGHT © JAMES G OLLÉ 1971
ALL RIGHTS RESERVED
0–208–01051–3

Z
721
O48
1971

CONTENTS

INTRODUCTION

The demand for a second edition of this book has given me the opportunity not only to draw attention to some of the more recent literature on library history, but to devote additional space to most of the topics covered.

Over the past three years, there have been several important additions to the published literature of British library history, among them the collected essays of Paul Kaufman, on the community libraries of the eighteenth century, a new biography of Antonio Panizzi, by Edward Miller, the first biography of James Duff Brown, by W A Munford, and a detailed history of our oldest private subscription library, the Leeds Library, by Frank Beckwith. Equally welcome are the reprints of the classic histories of Edward Edwards and Ernest Savage, the study of cathedral libraries by Beriah Botfield and of the classic reports on public libraries which will always be associated with the names of William Ewart, Sir Frederick Kenyon, W G Adams and Lionel McColvin.

The study of library history begins at home and often it stays there. The chapter on the literature of American library history has been included in the hope that British librarians may explore more fully an area of library history no less interesting than our own and one which is linked with our own, at several points.

The literature of library history is now expanding rapidly. The most helpful source of information on new publications, both books and periodical articles, is the journal *Library history*, which normally includes a general survey of recent literature in addition to its formal reviews of major works.

Reprints of older works on library history, and important source material, have been issued by several publishers, at home and abroad, in the last two or three years. I would like to draw attention to an important series of reprints inaugurated in 1969, namely, the ' CLW reprint series ' published by University Microfilms Ltd, in collaboration with the College of Librarianship, Wales.

The intention of this book remains unchanged. It has been written primarily for those reading library history for examination purposes, but—and hence the considerable expansion here of the first edition—I hope it may prove useful, also, to those whose interest in library history is not precisely regulated by the requirements of an examination syllabus.

JAMES G OLLÉ

CHAPTER ONE

THE STUDY OF LIBRARY HISTORY

Thirty years after his own major works on library history had been published, the late Dr Ernest Savage was invited to write the introduction to John Thornton's *The chronology of librarianship*. He then found himself considering, for the first time, 'Why should we study the history of libraries? How does it benefit us?'. 'I admit', he said, 'that I can't remember asking myself these questions until I began to write this introduction. I have always got so much pleasure from this study that questions about its utility never come to my mind.'

Sooner or later, questions about the utility of library history are bound to occur to those who study it. It has been found necessary to justify the study of history ever since recorded history began. Many of our distinguished modern historians have discussed the nature and purpose of history, some of them at great length. A notable exception is A J P Taylor, who has said 'Why has history, alone among the arts, to be justified by its practical purpose? Why cannot it be simply fun? The truth is that history enables us to understand the past better—no more and no less.'

Library history has been defended, in different ways, by three well-known library historians: W A Munford 'Our library inheritance' *Library review* XVII (130) Summer 1959 101-106, Raymond Irwin *The English library* (Allen & Unwin, 1966) chapter I, and Louis Shores 'The school librarian as historian' *School libraries* 18 (3) Spring 1969 9-16. Dr Munford suggests that 'The maturity of a profession may be judged—although there are of course other tests—by its pride in its own past'. Dr Shores believes that 'better performance today may be handicapped by our failure to look back more often; if for no other reason than to be sure that we are not repeating our old mistakes'.

Whether or not we may profit from the study of history, in the sense of learning to avoid the mistakes that have been made in the past, is an old debating point. Civilisation would hardly progress if we did not learn something. But circumstances change and what would have been the right course of action in the 1870's may not be the right course of action in the 1970's.

One value of library history needs little justification. Properly to understand the library world as it is today, one must know how it has reached its present state. Why, after more than a hundred years, does so much remain to be done with the public library service? Why is the library of the British Museum part of the museum? Why are the libraries of our modern universities so much smaller than the university libraries of the USA, of comparable age? Why has library co-operation, within its short history, become so complex? Why have the commercial circulating libraries, which were once so popular, almost entirely disappeared? Why do we regard James Duff Brown as one of our greatest librarians and why do we admire Sir Thomas Bodley, as a library benefactor, more than Andrew Carnegie?

There are several valid reasons why we should study library history, but I doubt whether anyone who questions its value will be convinced of its usefulness by argument. The study of library history begins as an act of faith. It is easier to believe that it is worth while than it is to prove it. M R Cutcliffe is not impressed by theoretical arguments. 'I prefer to think', he says, 'that the main reason why library history is studied is sheer interest' (M R Cutcliffe 'The value of library history' *Library review* XXI (4) winter 1967 193-196).

It cannot be denied that interest in library history is growing rapidly. Its present popularity as an examination subject may not be regarded as the best proof of this, but there are other indications. Notable among them is the expanding membership of the Library Association's Library History Group.

The Library History Group was founded in 1962, largely through the efforts of Dr W A Munford. The group exists primarily to unite members of the association interested in library history, through meetings, discussions and publications, but it also endeavours to encourage the study of library history as a discipline, to stimulate original research and to foster the preservation of records of library development. It can now claim about

1,000 members and already has a flourishing branch in the north of England. From 1963-1966 the group published an irregular *Newsletter*, but in 1967 this was replaced by an attractive, illustrated, half-yearly journal called *Library history.*

The study of library history is not easy. The difficulties should not be daunting, but they cannot be ignored.

Firstly, there is the problem of library terminology. An important feature of Thomas Kelly's *Early public libraries*, often ignored by students, is appendix I: ' Library nomenclature '. Over the years, the terms ' public library ', ' subscription library ' and ' circulating library ', among others, have been used in a variety of senses. Dr Kelly is the first British library historian to have paid special attention to this problem, and although his classification of libraries is open to some criticism (Dr Kaufman, for one, has objected to his use of the term ' endowed libraries '), much confusion that exists between students, tutors and examiners would be avoided if Dr Kelly's recommendations were generally accepted.

Secondly, the literature of library history is now extensive. It is also uneven in value and widely scattered. On some important topics there are no adequate published sources of information, or none conveniently accessible. In this subject, therefore, as in many others in librarianship, the student will have to rely, to some extent, on information provided by his lecturers. But he must be willing to extend his reading beyond two or three of the standard textbooks, bearing in mind that, on several topics, the best sources of information are uncollected articles in periodicals.

The third difficulty is perhaps the greatest. Ideally, library history should not be studied on its own, but always in relation to the relevant social, educational and publishing history. Few library histories provide this necessary background, and although there is no lack of books which could be used in support of library history studies, there may well be difficulty in finding the time to read them. Doubtless, in years to come, library school courses will be longer than they are now and more time will be available for ' background studies '. In the meantime, I hope that students whose knowledge of general history is poor will take note that, in embarking upon the study of library history, they will be handicapped from the start.

Over the past twenty years, an increasing number of librarians have become involved—if only for a short time—in research in library history. Some have worked as free agents, on topics of their own choice. Others have laboured under restrictions, *eg*, librarians who have felt obliged to write jubilee or centenary histories of their libraries, or librarians who have written theses suited to the requirements of their universities, or the LA.

Furthermore, students preparing for examinations in library history have been encouraged to undertake modest research projects. The benefit of this exercise, when it can be done under favourable conditions, need hardly be stated.

The advice which follows is provided mainly for those working on projects or theses. It is not intended to replace, but to reinforce, the advice which will certainly be given to students by their tutors and supervisors.

The choice of a subject may cause considerable difficulty. Often it happens that a student is anxious to undertake a piece of research which cannot be approved. There are several likely reasons for this, which the student may not appreciate. At one extreme, there are the topics of wide extension which are unsuitable because the source materials are so plentiful that the student would never be able to find the time to cope with them. At the other extreme, there are topics which cannot be safely pursued as it is doubtful whether anything useful would be found.

Most of the work done for projects and theses falls into two classes: the history of one particular library, or the biography of an important librarian or library benefactor. Although, generally speaking, topics of this kind are of the right scale, they may present difficulties, nevertheless.

The commonest difficulties relate to libraries which no longer survive. It is an aggravating fact that libraries which existed well within living memory may defeat investigation because their archives have gone astray, or have been destroyed. Thus it happens that a student who feels inclined to work on the history of a defunct subscription library, or the library of a mechanics' institute, may properly be deterred from doing so by his tutor, who knows, or suspects, that nothing of importance will be discovered.

The work done by Paul Kaufman on our eighteenth century community libraries shows that sometimes valuable information may be found where little was expected, but what Dr Kaufman and other independent scholars may do, with time enough to follow their own inclinations, a student should not attempt.

Investigating the history of an existing library is not always easy. I know of several libraries which cannot produce a complete set of useful records such as annual reports, press cuttings or even the libraries' own publications.

The study of local library history over the past 200 years would be greatly facilitated if the files of local newspapers in libraries were complete and indexed, but it seldom happens that they are.

I have found that students, when working on the history of a local library, are apt to ignore the general literature of librarianship, on the assumption that nothing concerning the library being investigated would be found in it, or that the library itself would have off-prints, clippings or photocopies of anything of importance. In my experience, this is seldom true. Although some libraries have existed for many years without any significant reference to them in the professional literature, it is unwise not to make a routine check.

There is no detailed and comprehensive bibliography of British library history, a deficiency which the LA Library History Group is endeavouring to remedy. It is therefore necessary to rely upon the general bibliographies of library literature. Details of these will be found in Robert L Collison *Bibliographies: subject and national* (Crosby Lockwood, third edition 1968). Unfortunately, these general bibliographies cannot be relied upon implicitly. In the first place, they do not record every item published in our professional journals. Secondly, they have ignored many useful articles published elsewhere, more particularly those published in the journals of other professions and in the journals of national

13

and local learned societies. Thirdly, they seldom draw attention to useful historical information embedded in books, although this is hardly to be expected.

When it is necessary to search the back files of our professional periodicals, by using their own indexes, it is an advantage to know beforehand what periods they cover. I have therefore provided below a list of the major British periodicals of librarianship, current and defunct, with their dates of publication. As the LA has published several periodicals, since it was founded in 1877, I have grouped them together.

LIBRARY ASSOCIATION JOURNALS OF LIBRARIANSHIP
For some years, the LA had great difficulty in publishing a journal entirely out of its own resources. In its early days, it was assisted by the American Library Association, which generously allowed it to share the *Library journal*. Later it was assisted by two of its own officers, Ernest C Thomas in respect of the *Library chronicle* and John MacAlister in respect of *The library*. The succession of LA journals of librarianship is as follows:

Library journal November 1877 to June 1882

The dates given are for the period during which the LJ was styled ' Official organ of the Library Associations of America and of the United Kingdom '.

Monthly notes of the Library Association January 1880 to December 1883

Library chronicle January 1884 to December 1888

The library January 1889 to December 1898

Library Association record January 1899 to date

Published monthly, except for the period 1923-1930, when it was published quarterly. Since January 1957, it has included a news-sheet supplement called *Liaison*.

Journal of librarianship January 1959 to date

The LA has also published the transactions and proceedings of its annual conferences, but as these have sometimes been published separately and sometimes with its journal, the bibliography of LA conferences is complicated. For details see under ' Library

Association of the United Kingdom ' in the *British union–catalogue of periodicals.*

The other British periodicals of librarianship are listed below in the order of their appearance:

Library assistant (Library Assistants' Association; from 1922 Association of Assistant Librarians) January 1898 to December 1952; continued as the *Assistant librarian* January 1953 to date

Library world July 1898 to date

Librarian August 1910 to December 1961

Report of the proceedings of the annual conference of Aslib 1925-1948; succeeded by *Aslib proceedings* January 1949 to date

Library review Spring 1927 to date

Journal of documentation (Aslib) January 1945 to date.

One would expect any project or thesis submitted by a librarian to be impeccable in at least one respect, namely, that it would be well documented. But many which have passed through my hands have been remarkably deficient. For guidance on this and other matters, I commend to all who are proposing to undertake research in library history G Kitson Clark *Guide for research students working on historical subjects* (CUP, second edition 1968).

PLAN OF THIS BOOK
This book is not intended as a history of libraries, but as a guide to the literature of library history, with special reference to Great Britain. In so far as I have provided a summary of certain developments in library history, I have done so only as a broad indication of the territory which the student must explore for himself and to make clear the relevance of the literature recommended.

No student will have time to read all the books and articles mentioned, but as students are often encouraged to explore one or two topics in depth, I have not confined my reading lists to the more obvious sources of information. Even so, I have had to be highly selective.

The history of libraries can be studied in several ways. One way is to study the history of each type of library in turn. As this is the easiest method for the novice, most of the ensuing chapters follow this pattern. However, as it is important to know the chronological development of libraries, I have provided, in chapter four, a brief summary of British library history from the Middle Ages to the present day. This may not convey much at first reading, but I hope students will return to it after they have studied the remaining chapters.

CHAPTER TWO

GENERAL LIBRARY HISTORY

Until the middle of the nineteenth century, very little work was done on the history of libraries. The first histories of any importance were those of Edward Edwards (1812-1886), whose massive volumes are rightly regarded as classics, despite their obvious defects. ' He was erudite and industrious ', said Richard Garnett, ' though not sufficiently discriminating. His works occupy a place of their own, and will always remain valuable mines of information ' (DNB). At the very least, they must be regarded as an extraordinary achievement, written as they were under great difficulties and with little hope of adequate financial reward.

Edwards' finest work was his *Memoirs of libraries* (1859), which covers in detail the library history of the western world from earliest times to the 1850's. The *Memoirs* were published in two large volumes, the entire work amounting to about 2,000 pages. The chapter synopses alone occupy fifty pages. Edwards had a characteristic style, but few literary graces. In the *Memoirs,* as in his other works, he retarded the narrative with unnecessary digressions, but he brought to light a tremendous amount of information, much of it derived from his own researches. Edwards was rightly proud of the *Memoirs.* In 1865 he published a supplement to it called *Libraries and founders of libraries,* and in his retirement he worked on a thorough revision of the *Memoirs,* which he did not live to complete. Before he died, however, he had arranged for the section on the Middle Ages to be printed. The sheets of this fragment were rescued by Thomas Greenwood, Edwards' first biographer, who had them bound and privately distributed in 1901. In 1964 a handsome facsimile reprint of the 1859 edition of the *Memoirs* was published by Burt Franklin (New York), and in 1968 a facsimile reprint of *Libraries and founders of libraries* was published by Gerard Th Van Heusden (Amsterdam).

If an edited edition of the *Memoirs* were to be published today, it would be as clustered with footnotes as the *Variorum Shakespeare*. But even as it stands the *Memoirs* are more than a curiosity. They repay reading, if only to discover Edwards' personal opinions of libraries and librarianship, vigorously expressed and often sensible and far-sighted.

For many years, Edwards' books were the only aid to the general study of library history, but because of their bulk and their increasing deficiencies it was felt, at the beginning of this century, that there was a need for a new and handier history of libraries.

Ernest A Savage's *The story of libraries and book-collecting* (Routledge, 1909) was a sound work by a conscientious library historian, but, probably because Savage attempted to cover too much ground in a small volume, it had only a modest success and was never revised. In his retirement, Dr Savage wrote an essay on his experiences as a library historian, in which he said ' The study of library history must be subsidized and supervised '. (Ernest A Savage ' Casual amateur in bibliography ' *Library Association record* 65 (10) October 1963 361-365).

Twenty years after Savage's book appeared, an excellent miniature history of libraries was published in a pamphlet series called ' Benn's sixpenny library ': Sir Frederic Kenyon *Libraries and museums* (Benn, 1930). As Director and Principal Librarian of the British Museum, Chairman of the Board of Education's Public Libraries Committee and as an authority on the book-word of ancient Greece and Rome, Sir Frederic had singular qualifications as a library historian, and his modest essay is still worth reading, if one can find it.

In 1925, a short but scholarly history of libraries by Alfred Hessel, Librarian, University of Göttingen, was published in Germany. Some years later it was translated into English and published in America, with a supplementary chapter by Reuben Peiss, the translator: Alfred Hessel *A history of libraries* (Scarecrow Press, 1950; Reuben Peiss memorial edition 1955). This is still useful for its sections on European library history.

The latest attempt to provide a universal history of libraries is Elmer D Johnson *A history of libraries in the western world*

(Scarecrow Press, 1965). This is a good, straightforward textbook by an author with long experience in teaching library history, but the chapters on modern library history are too heavily loaded with detail, and the bibliographies are neither as informative, nor as accurate, as they might have been. Nevertheless, this is a useful book, although more suitable for reference than for continuous reading.

For many years we have had authoritative outlines of library history in the large-scale general encyclopedias. To these outlines we can now add the articles on library history in the encyclopedias of librarianship.

Thomas Landau's *Encyclopaedia of librarianship* (Bowes & Bowes, third edition 1966) is little concerned with library history outside Great Britain, but there is an excellent general article by Raymond Irwin (see under ' Libraries, history ').

Library history will occupy a fair amount of space in the international encyclopedia of librarianship which is now in course of publication in America: Allen Kent and Harold Lancour (*eds*) *Encyclopedia of library and information science* (New York, Marcel Dekker, vol 1 1968).

John L Thornton *The chronology of librarianship* (Grafton, 1941) is a pioneer reference work on library history which still remains useful, even although it is much in need of revision. It was based on a thorough examination of the more important published sources of information available at the time, but since then the literature of library history has increased enormously.

CHAPTER THREE

ANCIENT LIBRARIES

There is a general feeling among librarians, which student librarians undoubtedly share, that the libraries of the ancient world are of little interest and of no relevance to the libraries of modern times. There is some justification for this attitude. Ancient library history is like a jigsaw from which most of the pieces are missing. Students of library history can add nothing to the picture by their own researches (a limitation which does not apply to the study of public library history), and, through lack of knowledge of the ancient world, most students are not competent to speculate on the nature of the missing pieces, or pass judgment on the speculations of library historians, such as Raymond Irwin, who have made a special study of ancient libraries.

A little knowledge of ancient history is essential before beginning the study of ancient libraries. For want of it, students are apt to glide through this part of their studies as quickly as they can, and in doing so are likely to telescope the events of more than 1,000 years into one vaguely located century.

If we are not too precise in our definition of ' library ', we can say that libraries are as old as civilisation. The earliest libraries, which were often attached to temples and cared for by priests, might be better described as record repositories.

We know little of the early libraries of Egypt, but thanks to the labours of archeologists and the survival of clay tablets we do know something about the palace and temple libraries of Babylonia and Assyria. To the library historian, the unearthing of the cuneiform clay tablets which formed part of the national library established at Nineveh, in the seventh century BC, by the Assyrian monarch Ashurbanipal, is as important and as interesting as the discovery of the remains of the Qumran library in the Dead Sea caves.

Where to place the beginning of Greek libraries depends upon what we are prepared to accept in the way of circumstantial evidence. There may have been private libraries in the fifth century BC, but there can be little doubt that in the fourth century there were libraries attached to three of the four great Athenian schools of philosophy. The best recorded is the library of the Peripatetic School of Aristotle (the Lyceum). This library had a curious history. After Aristotle's retirement, it passed from hand to hand until eventually it was taken to Rome.

It is with Aristotle's library that the continuous library history of the western world begins. It probably inspired the foundation of the great Museum and Library at Alexandria, which survived into the christian era. The museum was established in the third century BC by Ptolemy I, and was developed by his successors until it became one of the wonders of the ancient world. The museum was a literary and bibliographical research centre, and to serve it the library acquired a unique collection of Greek literature. (Although it is customary to speak of the Alexandrian Library, there were, in fact, two libraries, as Ptolemy III established a daughter library in the temple of Serapis.) The names of some of the head librarians have come down to us, but they are less familiar to us than the name of Callimachus, who was not head librarian, but a bibliographer.

The later history of the library is imperfectly known. The main library was destroyed in the third century AD and the Serapeum in AD 391. Thus we lost the greatest library the world had yet known, or was to know until modern times.

The rival library at Pergamum, in Asia Minor, was founded by Eumenes II in the second century BC. It existed for about 150 years. Although apparently a substantial library, it was far less important than the Alexandrian Library in the history of scholarship. It has often been stated that the Pergamum library pioneered the use of vellum as a writing material, and that the library itself was forcibly removed by Mark Antony to Alexandria, but these stories are of doubtful authenticity.

The earliest libraries of Rome were brought there in the second century BC as spoils of war. In the following century, there was an indigenous growth of private libraries in palaces and villas. There are references to the villa libraries in the letters of Cicero and the younger Pliny, and also in the well-known diatribe by Seneca, who fulminated against those who acquired libraries merely for show.

The first public library in Rome was founded *c* BC 37, during the reign of Augustus. By the fourth century AD, Rome reputedly had about thirty public libraries, but we know the names of only a few, and these were all reference libraries attached to temples. The villa libraries, some of which were quite large, were much more important in the history of scholarship than the public libraries, as they helped to preserve the Latin classics. Irwin has said that, if in place of the thirty or more public libraries Rome had been given one great national library, like the Library of Alexandria, ' the history of Western scholarship might well have been different' (*Encyclopedia of library and information science* vol 1 406).

Public and private libraries eventually appeared in the Roman provinces, but there is no direct evidence that any existed in Roman Britain.

The economy of Roman libraries was simple, and for a long time it was based on the papyrus roll. It was not until the fourth century AD that the codex came into general use.

After the fall of Rome, in the fifth century AD, its libraries fell into ruin and decay and archeologists have found little trace of them. The most spectacular discovery was made in 1752, when the remains of a small private library were discovered at Herculaneum.

It was during the first century BC, presumably, that the religious community at Qumran built up its library. The discovery of the scrolls in the Dead Sea caves was followed by a careful excavation of the remains of the pre-christian monastery where they originated. This unexpected addition to ancient library history stands apart from the rest.

Raymond Irwin's essays on the libraries of Greece, Alexandria and Rome, in his complementary books *The English library* and *The heritage of the English library,* are a well reasoned attempt to provide an ample and convincing account of libraries which are undoubtedly interesting, but for which we have few incontrovertible facts. Before reading these essays, students are advised to refer to Sir Frederic Kenyon's articles ' Books ' and ' Libraries ' in the *Oxford classical dictionary,* or to the summarised history of ancient libraries by Irwin in the *Encyclopaedia Britannica* (the first section of the article ' Library '), or in the *Encyclopedia of library and information science* vol 1 ('Ancient and medieval libraries ').

Other sources of information include J W Thompson *Ancient libraries* (University of California Press, 1940; Archon Books, 1962), Elmer D Johnson *A history of libraries in the western world* chapters 1-5 and J W Clark *The care of books* (CUP, second edition 1902) chapter I.

E A Parsons *The Alexandrian Library* (Elsevier, 1952) is a well-meant attempt to provide a full history of the library by bringing together every direct and oblique reference to it. If the author had disciplined himself to exclude from the text the mass of irrelevant and insignificant material, his book would have been more widely read than it is. In his final chapter, Parsons contends that part of the library survived until AD 646.

Useful sources of background information on the libraries of Greece and Rome are Sir Frederic Kenyon *Books and readers in ancient Greece and Rome* (OUP, second edition 1951) and L D Reynolds and N G Wilson *Scribes and scholars* (OUP, 1968), a study of the processes by which the texts of Greek and Latin literature have been preserved. See also C H Roberts ' The codex ' *Proceedings of the British Academy* 1954 169-204.

There is now a considerable literature on the Dead Sea scrolls. Those items particularly relevant to our studies include F M Cross *The ancient library of Qumran* (Duckworth, 1958) and K G Pedley *The library at Qumran* (Berkeley, Peacock Press, 1964), an interesting pamphlet in which the Qumran library is given its place in ancient library history.

From the ancient libraries of Greece and Rome we pass to the medieval libraries of Europe and so to the library history of Great Britain. It is at this point in our studies that Raymond

Irwin's books become of special interest and value. He identifies the links between the ancient libraries and the libraries of the Middle Ages, and he shows that the medieval libraries and scriptoria were influenced not only by Saint Benedict and his famous Rule, but also by the work of his great contemporary Cassiodorus, at the monastery he founded called the Vivarium. It should be noted that Irwin has added to *The English library* (the revised edition of *The origins of the English library*) an entirely new chapter ' The Byzantine age '.

CHAPTER FOUR

BRITISH LIBRARY HISTORY

There is no comprehensive monograph on British library history. The outline history which constitutes the first part of Albert A Predeek *A history of libraries in Great Britain and America* (ALA, 1947) is unsatisfactory. It was imperfect when it was published and it is now far behind recent researches in British library history.

The most useful work on British library history is Thomas Kelly *Early public libraries: a history of public libraries in Great Britain before 1850* (LA, 1966). This was written to pave the way for Dr Kelly's forthcoming history of the public library movement. Although Dr Kelly describes *Early public libraries* as no more than a preliminary survey, it is of unique value. It brings together information which was hitherto widely scattered, it incorporates the results of Dr Kelly's own researches into the history of parochial and quasi-parochial libraries and the history of the mechanics' institutes, and it directs the reader to many other sources of information. Although Dr Kelly was mainly concerned with libraries which were, or may have been, accessible to the public, *Early public libraries* covers most aspects of British library history from the Middle Ages to the first Public Libraries Act. It follows, therefore, that no one who is interested in British library history before 1850 can afford to ignore it. *Early public libraries* includes a fair amount of detail, however, and it is a boon to have a skilful summary of it in pamphlet form: Thomas Kelly *Public libraries in Great Britain before 1850* (LA, 1966).

Raymond Irwin's distinctive contribution to British library history is to be found in the two volumes of essays which have already been mentioned, namely, *The English library* (Allen & Unwin, 1966) and *The heritage of the English library* (Allen & Unwin, 1964). Between them these books provide a fairly continuous survey of British library history from Roman Britain to the early nineteenth century. Irwin's declared intention was to ' give vitality to the often meagre facts and set them in perspective against the development of our civilisation'. This he has done with such success that both books have had a cordial reception outside the library profession, as well as within it.

The English library before 1700 edited by Francis Wormald and C E Wright (Athlone Press, 1958) is based on a series of lectures delivered under the auspices of the School of Librarianship and Archives, University College, London. This is a book of outstanding importance, as each chapter is founded almost entirely on primary sources of information.

Our knowledge of British library history of the eighteenth century has been substantially enlarged, in recent years, by the researches of an American scholar, Paul Kaufman. Dr Kaufman is particularly interested in our 'community libraries', a useful term he has introduced to cover every type of local library intended for public use, whether freely, or by payment of a subscription. As Dr Kaufman's studies have been published in a wide variety of periodicals, on both sides of the Atlantic, the recent collection of them in book form should do much to make them better known: Paul Kaufman *Libraries and their users* (LA, 1969). Unfortunately, some of the essays have been abbreviated. The cuts have been most severe in the long and valuable essay entitled 'The community library: a chapter in English social history'. Students are therefore advised to read this in its original form in the *Transactions of the American Philosophical Society* new series 57 (7) October 1967.

English libraries 1800-1850 (H K Lewis, 1958) includes the text of three further lectures delivered at University College, London. The topics dealt with are Panizzi and the British Museum Library, George Birkbeck and mechanics' institutes, and Carlyle and the London Library.

The next three works to be mentioned may be described as companions for the study of British library history. The first is John L Thornton *The chronology of librarianship* (Grafton, 1941), which has already been described. The second is John L Thornton *Selected readings in the history of librarianship* (LA, 1966), a consolidation and enlargement of two previous books by the same author, namely, *A mirror for librarians* (Grafton,

1948) and *Classics of librarianship* (LA, 1957). The title of *Selected readings* is misleading. It is not, save incidentally, a collection of writings on library history, but an anthology of ' representative writings of men who have influenced the development of librarianship '. Forty nine distinguished librarians and library benefactors of the past are represented, most of them British. The selection from each author is preceded by a brief biography and bibliography by the editor. *Selected readings* provides extracts from several important early writings on librarianship which are now hard to find, and it serves, to some degree, as a retrospective biographical dictionary of librarians. I must also add that it is an excellent book to browse in.

The third companion may be described as a supplement to *Selected readings*. In 1906-1907, several early and rare works on librarianship were reprinted in the USA, in limited editions. These reprints have now been reprinted, in one volume: John Cotton Dana and Henry W Kent (*eds*) *Literature of libraries in the seventeenth and eighteenth centuries* (Scarecrow Reprint Corporation, 1967). In this volume will be found, among other things, the writings of Sir Thomas Bodley and James Kirkwood.

There are few full length biographies of British librarians and library benefactors and no formal biographical dictionary of them. Biographical information therefore has to be sought for in a variety of publications. The *Dictionary of national biography* has no subject index, and it is difficult to estimate how many librarians it includes. In the main part of the *Dictionary*, the coverage is certainly good, but few librarians have won a place in the supplementary volumes covering the present century. This defect is partly remedied by the volumes of *Who was who*.

Frederic Boase *Modern English biography* (which has a subject index) includes entries for about a hundred librarians who died in the period 1851-1900, but most of them are of minor importance.

John Minto *A history of the public library movement in Great Britain and Ireland* (LA, 1932) includes a biographical dictionary of ' prominent workers and benefactors ', in chapter XIX. Most of the brief biographical entries in Thomas Landau's *Encyclopaedia of librarianship* are for public librarians.

The only source of information on many British librarians is the obituary notices of them in the professional journals. These notices, and other biographical articles, may sometimes be traced in the general bibliographies of librarianship. It is advisable, however, to make an additional check of the indexes to the individual volumes of the periodicals of librarianship, as obituary notices have often been ignored by the general bibliographies.

Dr W A Munford has the distinction of being the only library historian to have specialised in biographical work. He has so far published biographies of William Ewart, Edward Edwards, James Duff Brown and (in collaboration with W G Fry) Louis Stanley Jast. Dr Munford has written a good humoured account of his exacting labours in ' Confessions of a library biographer ' *Library review* 21 (6) Summer 1968 293-297.

The library history of the British Isles has been unevenly explored. Far more has been written on the library history of England than that of Wales, Scotland or Ireland. In several respects, the library history of Scotland is of unique interest. This is readily apparent from the essays of Paul Kaufman and from W R Aitken *History of the public library movement in Scotland* (1955). Dr Aitken's detailed and fully documented history (his doctoral thesis) deals not only with the rate supported libraries, but also with the various community libraries which preceded them. Regrettably, this invaluable work has not been formally published, but Xerox and positive microfilm copies have been made available by the Microfilm Association of Great Britain.

There is little in the following pages on the library history of Ireland. This is not a deliberate slight, but an unavoidable omission. Much remains to be done on Irish library history and most of what has been published is either in the form of locally published pamphlets, or articles in the professional journals. Those who wish to explore Irish library history are advised to consult the general bibliographies of librarianship and the files of *An leabharlann* (the journal of the Library Association of Ireland), where they will find a number of valuable articles and references to other sources.

Many books could be used as background reading in the study of British library history. Students can readily discover useful titles for themselves, but the following may be especially commended: Ronald C Benge *Libraries and cultural change* (Bingley, 1970), Richard Altick *The English common reader: a social history of the mass reading public 1800-1900* (University of Chicago Press, 1957; paper edition 1963), Thomas Kelly *A history of adult education in Great Britain* (Liverpool University Press, 1962) and Raymond Williams *The long revolution* (Chatto & Windus, 1961; Penguin 1965).

It is a matter for reflection that the social histories of Great Britain have little or nothing to say about libraries. One exception is R J Mitchell, and M D R Leys *A history of the English people* (Longmans, 1950; Pan Books 1967).

CHRONOLOGY OF BRITISH LIBRARY HISTORY
As the chapters which follow deal with the history of types of libraries, I have provided below a brief chronological survey, with the warning that students will only find it of value if they fill it out for themselves as their studies progress.

Roman Britain: In April 1960, the remains of a large Roman palace were discovered at Fishbourne, in Sussex. But neither here, nor anywhere else, have any traces been discovered of a library which existed during the Roman occupation. 'I suppose', said Raymond Irwin, 'that the average historian of libraries would omit any chapter on the libraries of Roman Britain'. Having said this, Irwin argues persuasively that there were libraries during this period, although 'there is no direct evidence that any existed' (*The English library* chapter V).

Middle Ages: 'The history of libraries in the Middle Ages', said Sir Frederic Kenyon, 'is the history, painfully gathered from scanty evidence, of collections of books in monasteries, their gradual growth and multiplication, and eventually the spread of the habit of forming such collections to colleges and private owners' (*Libraries and museums* 14).

Although the history of the medieval English monasteries covers about 1,000 years, their collections of books grew very slowly, and few houses ever acquired what we would now describe as a library. But although the monastic book collections seldom exceeded a few hundred volumes, they were highly prized and carefully guarded.

To Kenyon's observation on the libraries of the Middle Ages we must add Thomas Kelly's: 'It is not as generally known that libraries, or at least collections of books, were to be found also in the secular cathedrals, in collegiate churches, in parish churches, and even, towards the close of the Middle Ages, in a few schools' (*Early public libraries* 14-15).

Sixteenth century: The sixteenth century was a bleak period in our library history. The dispersal of the monastic books, in the reign of Henry VIII, was followed by the drastic purging of the libraries of the cathedrals and universities in the reign of Edward VI.

The opportunity to found a national library with books from the monasteries was lost, but in the latter part of the century some of the books were retrieved by private collectors, such as Archbishop Parker. The latter part of the century also saw the provision of a few endowed libraries in churches and schools.

Seventeenth century: Despite the Civil War, which brought damage and destruction to several cathedral and private libraries, the seventeenth century was a period of modest but almost continuous library progress, chiefly notable for the establishment of further endowed libraries, most of which were in towns. Unfortunately, most of these libraries were not endowed, in the sense of being given permanent means of support, but there were two well-known exceptions. One of them was Chetham's Library, Manchester, a free public reference library, and the other the Bodleian Library, Oxford. Sir Thomas Bodley offered to restore the library of Oxford University in 1598. When he died, in 1613, his new library was already firmly established and soon it became one of the finest libraries in Europe. It was the first library in Britain to benefit from deposited books and, until the foundation of the British Museum Library, it was, in effect, the national library of England. At the end of the century, the newly established library of the Faculty of Advocates, at Edinburgh, was making good progress, and for many years it served as the national library of Scotland, which it eventually became, by Act of Parliament, in 1925.

The foundation of the Royal Society, in 1660, was soon followed by the establishment of a library, an event commonly regarded as a landmark in the history of special libraries.

Eighteenth century: At the beginning of the eighteenth century, zealous attempts were made by Thomas Bray to increase the number of parochial libraries, but although, after his death, his work was continued by a trust called the Associates of Dr Bray, his ambitious scheme for a nation-wide network of parochial libraries, including both 'fixed' and lending libraries, was never realised.

In Scotland, the even more ambitious scheme of James Kirkwood to establish parish libraries for the use of both clergy and parishioners, came to nothing, but his later proposal to establish parochial libraries in the Highlands had a temporary success.

The middle of the century saw the belated foundation of a national library. The Library of the British Museum was opened to the public in 1759, but it did not become a really effective library until the following century.

Taking the country as a whole, the most important development in the eighteenth century was the introduction and rapid development of subscription libraries, most of which were founded by, or for, the gentry. Early in the century, commercial subscription libraries (circulating libraries) were provided by various booksellers. These libraries rapidly grew in numbers when the novel became a popular literary form. By the end of the century there were reputedly 1,000 of them.

The early part of the century also saw the formation of the first book clubs. The membership of a book club was small—from ten to thirty members. With a society of something more than 100 members it was possible to establish a permanent library, and in the latter part of the century private subscription libraries were successfully established in many of the larger towns in the provinces.

Nineteenth century: By 1800, there was a fair number of libraries in England, but most of the endowed libraries had fallen into decay, and most of the libraries which flourished were subscription libraries for the gentry. The Select Committee on Public Libraries (1849) investigated the former, but ignored the latter. But the committee was very much interested in the libraries of the mechanics' institutes, which were, in effect, cheap subscription libraries for the working classes. The MI movement, which began in the 1820's, never entirely realised its intentions. In a few of the larger towns the institutes were well supported and their libraries became large enough to provide for a wide range of interests, but by the end of the century the combined effects of the Education Acts and the Public Libraries Acts had swept most of the MIS out of existence.

The first Public Libraries Act (1850) is one of the greatest events in library history, but this Act, like all the other Public Libraries Acts before the 1964 Act, was permissive. Until the 1870's, the rate of adoptions was slow, but by the end of the century the efforts of national and local supporters of the movement and the greater need for public libraries following the Education Acts had led to the establishment of ' free libraries ' in most of the larger towns.

Public libraries had no immediate effect on subscription libraries. By the end of the century the private subscription libraries began to dwindle in numbers, but the circulating libraries attracted even more subscribers. Mudie's Select Library, founded in 1842, became a great Victorian institution and W H Smith started the first chain of circulating libraries at his railway bookstalls.

The century also saw the foundation of many institutional libraries, in particular the libraries of national and local learned societies and the libraries of the new professional associations. The libraries of the new ' redbrick ' universities and university colleges made slow progress, as they had no regular support from the government until the present century.

The latter half of the century saw an appreciable increase in the literature of librarianship, and the foundation of the first library associations. The Library Association of the United Kingdom (to give it its original title) was founded in 1877 and the Library Assistants' Association in 1895.

As the century drew to a close, despite the many difficulties with which they had to contend, the librarians of the public and institutional libraries had reason to feel proud and hopeful. Among the many interesting features of this remarkable century is the considerable increase in the number of libraries in London. Progress was sometimes difficult, however. The peculiarities of local government hindered the establishment and development of public libraries; it was not until 1841, when the London Library was founded, that the metropolis had a permanent private subscription library; and Panizzi's re-organisation of the British Museum Library was accomplished in the face of unremitting criticism and personal vilification.

Twentieth century: In the early years of the present century, the number of national public libraries increased from one to three. The efforts of the Welsh people made the National Library of Wales a reality and the magnificent library of the Faculty of Advocates, at Edinburgh, was reluctantly taken over by the government, as a gift, to become the National Library of Scotland.

At the beginning of the century, Andrew Carnegie gave substantial aid to the public library movement, with the result that many small local authorities hastily adopted the Acts to secure a free library building.

In 1913, Carnegie established the Carnegie United Kingdom Trust, which lent its support to the campaign for the removal of parliamentary restriction on the library rate and used its own resources to finance experimental rural library services. But despite the help of the CUKT, the county libraries which were officially established after the Public Libraries Act 1919 were unable to provide more than a token service, and during the inter-war period only a few municipal libraries benefited from the removal of rate restriction. Public librarians were understandably proud of the national-regional system of library co-operation which they brought into being in the 1930's but co-operation revealed poverty, as well as relieving it.

The belated realisation that British industry needed to invest in research and development brought into being the first industrial libraries, but not many were established in the inter-war period. The Association of Special Libraries and Information Bureaux (Aslib) was founded in 1924, but for some years it had a precarious existence.

The University Grants Committee, founded in 1919, gave university libraries much needed help, but the libraries of the ' redbrick universities ' made slow progress until the 1950's.

It was during the years of the depression, which restricted the activities of many libraries, that the LA achieved financial stability. With financial help from the CUKT, and co-operation from the Association of Assistant Librarians, the LA entered the 1930's much stronger than it had ever been.

The years immediately following the second world war saw a marked increase in the number of special libraries, soon to be followed by an increase in the number of university libraries and the libraries of vocational colleges. Meanwhile, hindered by building and other restrictions, public libraries marked time and waited hopefully for a new Public Libraries Act. It was the public library service, however, which obtained the greatest benefit from the system of full-time professional education which developed after 1946, when the first of the post-war schools of librarianship were established.

The 1960's were such eventful years that the contributors to a symposium on library progress during this decade (*The library world* December 1969) had great difficulty in bringing all the events into focus. Although the commercial circulating libraries almost entirely disappeared, with the closure of the libraries operated by Smith's and Boots' and the few remaining private subscription libraries found themselves facing a bleak and uncertain future, most other libraries made good progress, even while they were complaining that they could not progress fast enough. Library historians of the future may well look back upon the 1960's as the decade of reports. During the 1960's, there was more hard thinking about principles and policies than ever before. Reports on the public library service were followed by reports on the university libraries, and these by a highly controversial report on the British Museum Library. It was during this decade, also, that the terms ' library standards ' and ' research in librarianship ' first became common currency.

CHAPTER FIVE

MONASTIC LIBRARIES

Medieval library history extends from the sixth century to the fifteenth century. One could say, as Irwin does, that it has a precise beginning when St Benedict founded his monastery at Monte Cassino. Throughout this long period, almost all the libraries of western Europe were institutional and ecclesiastical— the libraries of the monasteries and the cathedrals.

By 'monastic libraries' we really mean the collections of books in the religious houses. The essential point is not that monastery means 'a community of monks', and is therefore narrower in application than 'religious house', but that 'the monastic library was not a library at all, if by a library is understood a building housing a collection of books' (David Knowles).

Before the Norman conquest, monasteries were comparatively few in England and their development was hindered by the Danish invaders who frequently plundered the monasteries and sometimes killed the monks. The early libraries founded at Jarrow and Wearmouth in the seventh century and at York in the eighth century were outstanding in their day, but they did not survive very long.

Although, after the Norman conquest, monasteries increased both in numbers and in wealth, their book collections grew very slowly. Most houses were small and so had neither the need nor the means to acquire many books. By the dissolution, even the libraries of the larger houses were small by modern standards. To a medieval monastery a mere 1,000 volumes (which meant rather more than 1,000 titles) was a substantial collection.

The nucleus of a monastic library was the necessary service books and the scriptures. To these were added books for teaching, practical works on law, medicine and husbandry and books for devotional purposes.

The collections grew in three ways: by copying books borrowed from other houses, by occasional purchases and by gifts and bequests. The most substantial acquisitions were most likely to come by gift. The growth of a monastic library was haphazard.

Dr Savage said that the spirit of modern librarianship is first traceable in the monasteries, particularly in the libraries of the larger houses such as Canterbury, Dover, Bury St Edmunds and Syon. But even in these houses the library economy was simple. The traditional design of a monastery did not allow for any particular accommodation for books. Those not in use were mostly kept in the cloister, in chests, presses or wall-cupboards. Several of the larger houses eventually built book rooms, but the first of these did not appear until the beginning of the fifteenth century.

The duties of librarian were performed by the precentor, whose particular concern was to see that the books were not damaged or lost. Librarianship in the medieval monasteries was librarianship in slow motion. The loan of books within a monastery was commonly an annual procedure and, as far as we know, books were seldom lent outside. J W Clark's observation that the monastic libraries were 'the public libraries of the Middle Ages' has often been quoted, but Clark was speaking of European monasteries generally and not of the English monasteries specifically (J W Clark *The care of books* 55, 64). Kelly has discussed, at length, how far the English monastic libraries were accessible to the public. He concludes that although books were occasionally lent to outsiders and were 'reasonably accessible for purposes of reference', few laymen were either able or willing to make use of them.

The end of the eleventh century saw the foundation of the first of several new religious orders, which soon established houses in this country. Among these reformed orders, the Cistercian order is of special interest, as the Cistercians are supposed to have paid particular attention to the problem of housing books.

In the thirteenth century, the pioneer mendicant orders came to England, the Dominicans in 1221 and the Franciscans in 1224. The friars were dedicated to poverty, but to sustain their work of teaching and preaching they soon found it necessary to erect their own conventual buildings and to provide themselves with their own collections of books. In the fourteenth century, Richard de Bury, in his *Philobiblon*, accused the friars of being zealous book-collectors, but K W Humphreys, who has recently made an intensive study of the book collections of the friars, says that ' The collections of books were not made in any spirit of covetousness or pride in accumulation, but for the equipment of the friars in their studies' (*The book provisions of the mediaeval friars* 89).

The Franciscans found a staunch patron in Robert Grosseteste, Bishop of Lincoln. ' It was largely his influence that guided them forward from their founder's rejection of learning and books into the paths of academic studies' and encouraged them to collect books (Irwin).

After about a hundred years the friars lost their popularity with the people, but by that time they had achieved great influence at the new universities, especially at Oxford (see *The heritage of the English library* chapter IX).

The dissolution of the monasteries (1536-1540), when about 800 houses were suppressed, led to the wanton dispersal of their books. The patient labours of modern scholars (notably the late Dr M R James) have shown that the number of books destroyed was not altogether so great as was once supposed, but the proportion of books lost from some houses was much greater than from others. Thus, 560 volumes survive from the library of the Cathedral Priory of Durham, but only fifteen volumes from the large library of Leicester Abbey.

As the monastic libraries were ' special libraries' rather than ' public libraries', few laymen regretted their passing. When the monasteries were dissolved in France, at the end of the eighteenth century, special pains were taken to secure the books for the benefit of the national library and various local libraries. Although Henry VIII was advised to enrich the Royal Library with monastic books, not many were acquired. Fortunately, it was still possible, later in the century, for several private collectors to obtain monastic volumes of unique interest, books which eventually found a permanent home in the libraries of Oxford and Cambridge and the British Museum Library.

The monastic libraries having been dispersed, the future of librarianship lay with other institutional libraries and increasingly with libraries of printed books. Not many printed books were acquired by the monasteries. An interesting exception is the library of the solitary English house of the Bridgettines, at Syon, founded in 1415.

It is unlikely that much more will be discovered about the English monastic libraries, and we are badly in need of a new monograph on them. Ernest A Savage *Old English libraries* (Methuen, 1911; reprinted Gale Research Company, 1968) is still of some value, as David Knowles acknowledges, but it is a difficult book for students without any previous knowledge of the subject.

The most useful introductory readings are Francis Wormald and C E Wright *(eds) The English library before 1700* (University of London Athlone Press, 1958) chapters II, V and VIII, and the chapters on the monastic libraries in the standard works on English monasticism by David Knowles, namely, *The monastic order in England* (CUP, 1940) 522-527 and *The religious orders in England* vol II (CUP, 1955) 331-353. See also Thomas Kelly *Early public libraries* chapters I and II and Raymond Irwin *The heritage of the English library* chapter VIII and *The English library* chapters VI, VII and VIII.

Until recent years, little work had been done on the libraries of the friars, and convenient readings on this subject are few. The most important study is K W Humphreys *The book provisions of the mediaeval friars 1215-1400* (Amsterdam, Erasmus Booksellers, 1964), but the references to the English libraries of the mendicants are scattered. Irwin's essay ' S. Robert of Lincoln and the Oxford Greyfriars' will be found in *The heritage of the English library* chapter IX.

Not many catalogues of monastic libraries have survived. Good examples of those which have been transcribed and published are M R James *The ancient libraries of Canterbury and Dover* (CUP, 1903) and Mary Bateson *Catalogue of the library of Syon monastery* (CUP, 1898). N R Ker *Medieval libraries of Great Britain* (Royal

Historical Society, second edition 1964) is a location list of surviving monastic books, with an informative preface.

The story of the monastic libraries of Britain is part of the medieval library history of Europe. See J W Thompson *The medieval library* (University of Chicago Press, 1939; reprinted Hafner 1957).

CHAINED LIBRARIES

In the latter part of the middle ages, the practice of chaining books became common. As Canon Streeter has said, this is not ' an interesting irrelevance ' in library history, but an important matter for consideration, as the chaining of books dominated library design for many years. After the dissolution, books were chained in the cathedral libraries and in the university and college libraries of Oxford and Cambridge. At Oxford, some libraries were still using chains in the eighteenth century.

The standard treatise on this subject is B H Streeter *The chained library* (Macmillan, 1931), a splendidly illustrated volume inspired by the author's labours on the restoration of the famous chained library at Hereford Cathedral. See also Wormald and Wright chapter XI, which discusses the use of chains at Oxford.

CHAPTER SIX

CATHEDRAL AND PAROCHIAL LIBRARIES

CATHEDRAL LIBRARIES: Thomas Kelly has said that the story of our cathedral libraries 'has been strangely neglected'. This is not altogether true, for over the past century a good deal has been published on individual cathedral libraries, but until Kelly himself turned his attention to cathedral library history, in his *Early public libraries,* no one had attempted a general survey.

Before the dissolution of the monasteries, there were two types of cathedrals, monastic and secular. The former served a double purpose—they were monastic churches as well as cathedrals. The latter were served by chapters of secular canons.

Although the libraries of the secular cathedrals were small, Kelly finds them of special interest because the books were more conveniently accessible, and, in their latter years, as chained reference libraries, they were closer than the monastic libraries 'to the modern concept of a public library'.

The purging of libraries which took place in the mid sixteenth century, to remove 'superstitious and Popish books', affected some cathedral libraries more than others. About a third of them managed to retain a substantial number of their medieval books.

Ironically, the purging coincided with an injunction to the deans and chapters that 'they shall maike a librarie in some convenient place within the space of one yeare next'.

Since then, the growth of cathedral libraries has been haphazard and generally slow. It has always been difficult to find money to buy books, and the libraries which have grown most since the sixteenth century are those which have been fortunate in their benefactors.

The seventeenth century brought both good and ill fortune to cathedral libraries. Several were damaged, or destroyed, during the Civil War (for example, Chichester, Exeter and Peterborough), and the libraries of Old St Paul's and Lincoln were accidentally destroyed by fire.

41

2*

For the most part, however, destruction was soon followed by zealous restoration. An exception was Chichester, where the library destroyed in 1642, when the cathedral was sacked, was not replaced until 1750.

When community libraries were few, one might have expected the cathedral libraries to have been specially useful, but for various reasons they were not. Most of them were fairly small and until the latter part of the nineteenth century many were neglected and access to them was difficult.

A few years ago, Paul Kaufman discovered that eight of the old cathedral libraries (Canterbury, Carlisle, Durham, Exeter, Gloucester, Winchester, York and St Paul's) still retained their loan records for the eighteenth century. Kaufman's detailed analysis of these shows that, altogether, these eight libraries were used by 825 borrowers, of which no more than 15 percent were 'outsiders'. (Since Kaufman made his survey the loan records of Lichfield cathedral have come to light.)

For the nineteenth century, we have several useful sources of information. It happened, by chance, that in the middle of the century the cathedral libraries were subjected to three independent investigations. The first was by the bibliographer Beriah Botfield (1807-1863), who visited all the cathedral libraries and presented his findings in a book called *Notes on the cathedral libraries of England* (1849). Botfield was more interested in the stock of the libraries than in their history, but he provides some historical information and mentions several instances of destruction and serious neglect. The second investigation was by Edward Edwards, who reported on cathedral libraries to the Select Committee on Public Libraries (1849) and later described them more fully in his *Memoirs of libraries* (1859). The third investigation was by the Royal Commission on the state and condition of the cathedral and collegiate churches of England and Wales (1852), which provided information on cathedral libraries in its reports.

From these various sources, we learn that the cathedral libraries were small, their stocks heavily theological, their incomes negligible and public access to them often difficult. By 1878, when an excellent account of the cathedral libraries was presented to the

LA conference by Canon H E Reynolds (librarian of Exeter cathedral), there had been some improvement. Since then, despite continuing financial difficulties, a good deal has been done to repair the books and improve the accommodation of all the cathedral libraries. As Neil Ker points out, much of the credit for this must be given to a number of devoted cathedral librarians.

In 1966, the LA appointed a special committee to investigate the condition of the cathedral libraries. The committee's report (which has only been published in the form of a brief summary) was reassuring. It said that ' the libraries are admirably administered and cared for, and that cathedral authorities welcome scholars, and other persons requiring to use them, without undue formality ' (*LA annual report 1967* 17).

The importance of cathedral libraries was well expressed by Beriah Botfield, who wrote: ' The libraries thus preserved have, as might be expected, great similarity of character. They often combine in a peculiar manner the learning of the middle ages, with the literature of a later date. Chiefly embracing theological subjects, they contain no small amount of classical lore, and a large proportion of historical research. Among much that is obsolete there is more that is valuable, and amid much that is trifling there is more that is important ' (*Notes on the cathedral libraries of England* viii).

Unfortunately, there is no general monograph on cathedral libraries comparable to the magnificent *Parochial libraries of the Church of England* (which will be described later in this chapter), but an excellent brief survey has recently been published which serves as an admirable introduction to cathedral library history: N R Ker ' Cathedral libraries ' *Library history* Autumn 1967 1 (2) 38-45. There are several references to the history of cathedral libraries up to the mid nineteenth century in Thomas Kelly's *Early public libraries;* see, in particular, 58-67, 191-192.

On cathedral libraries in the eighteenth century see Paul Kaufman *Libraries and their users* chapter V, and in the nineteenth century Edward Edwards *Memoirs of libraries*, Beriah Botfield *Notes on the cathedral libraries of England* (Chiswick Press, 1849; reprinted Gale Research Co, 1969), and H E Reynolds ' Our cathedral libraries' *Transactions and proceedings of the first annual meeting of the LA* 1878 32-43.

Separate histories have been published of most of the older cathedral libraries, but the majority of them are not readily accessible (see the list in *Early public libraries* 67). The following references are restricted to those which may be consulted without much difficulty.

Canterbury: M Beazeley 'History of the Chapter Library of Canterbury Cathedral' *Transactions of the Bibliographical Society* VIII 1904-1906 113-185.

Durham: M Johnson 'Durham Cathedral Library' *Library Association record* 66 (9) September 1964 388-390.

Hereford: B H Streeter *The chained library* (Macmillan, 1931) chapters II and VI and Maura Tallon 'Hereford Cathedral Library' *An leabharlann* 20 (4) December 1962 130-142.

Lincoln: D N Griffiths 'Lincoln Cathedral Library' *Book collector* Spring 1970 19(1) 21-30.

Wells: T W Williams 'Wells Cathedral Library' *Library Association record* 8 August 1906 372-377.

Worcester: J. M. Wilson 'The library of printed books in Worcester Cathedral' *Library* third series II (5) January 1911 1-33.

PAROCHIAL LIBRARIES

Until the latter part of the nineteenth century, many of the parish clergy had great difficulty in obtaining books. They were too poor to buy them and they lived remote from good libraries which were either freely accessible or cheap to subscribe to. The clergy in the rural areas were the most unfortunate. Many of them had no convenient library service until the county libraries were established.

The cathedral libraries were never of much help to the parish clergy. Even if they were close at hand, they were open only for a few hours each week and the books the parish clergy wanted were not always available for loan.

It is probable that by the fifteenth century most churches had a few books other than service books, but at the Reformation they were discarded.

In the reign of Elizabeth I, parochial libraries were provided at Leicester, Bury St Edmunds, Newcastle, Ipswich and Grantham. Further libraries were provided during the seventeenth century, but by 1700 there were less than a hundred and most of these were in towns.

Although private benefactors continued to provide parochial libraries until the early years of the nineteenth century, from the beginning of the eighteenth century their efforts were augmented by the work of three national societies, which came into existence partly, or wholly, through the activities of Dr Thomas Bray (1656-1730).

Bray was an intelligent and energetic country clergyman who came to the notice of the Bishop of London and was employed by him to investigate the condition of the church in the colony of Maryland. Having reported that there was a great lack of books in the colony, Bray was encouraged to organise libraries there, a task he performed with zeal and success, not only in Maryland but in other British settlements in North America. But when he was reminded that there was equal need for books for the impoverished clergy at home, he characteristically turned his attention to the provision of parochial libraries in England and Wales. Although he provided a few libraries as a private benefactor, his personal resources were slender, and the majority of what are commonly called the Bray libraries were provided by one or other of the three societies with which he was connected.

The first was the Society for the Promotion of Christian Knowledge (1699). In 1702, the SPCK appointed a special committee to deal with the problem of libraries for the clergy. Presumably because it had several other responsibilities, the SPCK confined its library work to the provision of clerical lending libraries in Wales. Thereafter, the work was continued, throughout the rest of Bray's lifetime, by an independent committee called the Trustees for Erecting Parochial Libraries, established by Bray in 1705.

The trustees' libraries were small and more or less uniform collections of about seventy volumes. Kelly calls them 'fixed' libraries, as they were for the exclusive use of the incumbents of the parishes to which they were sent.

Soon after Bray died, the trustees disbanded and their work was taken over by another trust, the Associates of Dr Bray, which had been established in 1725 to provide negro schools in British America.

Bray estimated that there were 2,000 parishes where the livings were so poor that the clergy could hardly be expected to provide themselves with books. If this was a true estimate, then it is obvious that, when Bray died, the united efforts of the SPCK, the trustees and private benefactors had barely come to grips with the problem. It is clear, however, from Bray's several publications concerning parochial libraries, that he not only hoped for many more libraries, but libraries which were larger and more varied in stock than those which were actually provided under his direction. If his proposals could have been carried out, England and Wales would have been covered by a network of parochial libraries, both fixed and lending libraries.

The modest aim of the trustees was to provide two fixed libraries in each diocese, but ' some Bishops entertaining the Proposal very coldly ', the 66 libraries provided were distributed unevenly.

' Bray is a striking instance ', wrote Canon Overton, ' of what a man may effect without any extraordinary genius, and without special influence ' (DNB). This verdict is based on a study of his entire labours for the church, which were considerable. In assessing his library activities, it must be remembered that it was through no fault of his own that what was accomplished during his lifetime was a good deal less than he envisaged. Like James Kirkwood and Samuel Brown, he saw very clearly what needed to be done, but could never obtain sufficient financial support to carry out his plans.

Bray died in 1730. Within a few weeks of his death the trustees disbanded and their library responsibilities were taken over by the Associates of Dr Bray. The library work of the associates did not begin until 1753, but it then proceeded energetically. From 1753 to 1768, the associates were mainly concerned with fixed libraries, but from 1769 to 1803 they provided lending libraries only. This was a sensible change of policy, as it meant that the modest funds available to the associates could be used to greater effect. Strangely, they resumed the provision of fixed libraries in 1804 and provided both fixed and lending libraries until 1840, after which they again concentrated on lending libraries. Although the library activities of the associates have been investigated by Kelly, our knowledge of them is still imperfect. It would be interesting to know how much the lending libraries were used.

The libraries provided by private benefactors were generally larger and more interesting than those of the Bray societies. They often included works on history, literature and other subjects and sometimes volumes of considerable value.

The libraries provided by private benefactors, the SPCK, and The Trustees for Erecting Parochial Libraries, were outright gifts. As such, their preservation by the churches to which they were given was obligatory under the Act for the Better Preservation of Parochial Libraries 1708, a measure which had been passed at Bray's suggestion. The libraries distributed by the associates, however, were not given away, but provided on indefinite loan. The advantage of this arrangement was that they could be recalled by the associates when they had outlived their usefulness.

The associates still exist, and their library work continues, but since the latter part of the nineteenth century the need for parochial libraries has been much less urgent than it was in Bray's lifetime. Very few libraries were provided by private benefactors after 1800. Most parochial libraries were derelict when a report on them was submitted to the Ewart Committee in 1849.

Despite the provisions of the 1708 Act, parochial libraries were not only allowed to fall into decay, but several were sold or destroyed. In 1900, the *Church times* published an article lamenting the state of the Bray libraries and advanced the not very practical suggestion that the associates should employ an inspector of parochial libraries. A few years ago official action was taken to secure the preservation of such books as remained.

In 1949, at the instigation of the Bibliographical Society, the Archibishop of Canterbury asked the Central Council for the Care of Churches to enquire into the state of the old parochial libraries. The central council appointed a special investigating committee, whose report and recommendations were published in *The parochial libraries of the Church of England* (Faith Press, 1959). This handsome, illustrated volume, which was edited for the committee by Dr Neil Ker, is the principal source of information on our old parochial libraries. In addition to the committee's report, it includes a long historical introduction, the text of the Act and a most informative 'Alphabetical list of parochial libraries, past and present'. As Kelly points out, however, the historical introduction does not mention the trustees, and the libraries which they provided are credited to the SPCK. Furthermore, the libraries of the associates are entirely ignored, for the sufficient reason that the committee was only concerned with those libraries which were the absolute property of the churches which had them, the libraries which were protected by the Act. Therefore, although *The parochial libraries of the Church of England* is invaluable, it must be studied in association with Kelly's *Early public libraries* chapters IV and V and appendices II and III. The appendices provide what must be a nearly complete list of all the parochial libraries which existed before 1850, including the libraries of the associates.

The general history of parochial libraries has been sketched in Raymond Irwin *The heritage of the English library* chapter XIII, which pays particular attention to the pre-eighteenth century libraries. There is a good modern biography of Bray: H P Thompson *Thomas Bray* (SPCK, 1954). See also George Smith ' Dr Thomas Bray' *Library Association record* XII May 1910 242-260 and the DNB. On Bray and the SPCK see W K Lowther Clarke *A history of the SPCK* (SPCK, 1959) 77-80. ' The Bray clerical libraries' *Library Association record* III January 1901 29-31 is a reprint of the article in the *Church times,* referred to above.

Anyone who wishes to see a good English parochial library, in its original quarters, may have to travel a long way to do so. In *The parochial libraries of the Church of England* 26 and 58-59 there are details of many parochial libraries which have been sold, accidentally or deliberately destroyed, or which have disappeared for reasons unknown. In recent years, at least a third of the surviving libraries have been transferred, for safer keeping and greater use, to cathedral, university or public libraries, or county record offices. Among the interesting libraries which have not been removed, and are unlikely to be, are those at Grantham, Hereford (All Saints), Langley Marish and Wimborne Minster.

Histories and descriptions have been published of several individual parochial libraries, mostly as articles in the journals of learned societies. For details see the alphabetical list in the *Parochial libraries of the Church of England.*

PAROCHIAL LIBRARIES OF SCOTLAND

The parochial libraries of Scotland are more interesting with regard to what was proposed, rather than what was achieved. In 1699, the Rev James Kirkwood (*c* 1650-1708) published an anonymous tract called *An overture for establishing of bibliothecks in every paroch throughout this kingdom*, in which he presented a detailed and ambitious plan by which a system of parochial libraries might be established throughout the whole of Scotland. The scheme proposed involved the establishment of a central bureau with its own publishing house to publish cheap reprints of standard works, and the levying of a special library tax on each parish.

Kirkwood's proposal was addressed to the General Assembly of the Church of Scotland, which evidently found it impractical, for it took no steps to implement it. In 1702, Kirkwood published a second tract, in which he made the more reasonable suggestion that parochial libraries should be established in the Highlands, where books were particularly scarce. This proposal bore fruit. Over the period 1704-1709, the general assembly passed a series of measures which brought into being a number of small libraries in the Highland presbyteries and parishes, but how these libraries operated and how much they were used we do not know. Some of these libraries were reputedly destroyed during the rebellions of the eighteenth century, and all of them were either derelict or destroyed by the beginning of the nineteenth century.

When Kirkwood published the *Overture* he obviously had in mind a system of libraries under church control, but for the use of both clergy and parishioners. (Kelly suggests that libraries under parochial control, but ' designed for the use of inhabitants of the parish ', should be called parish libraries.)

The story of the Kirkwood libraries, as far as it is known, will be found in W R Aitken *History of the public library movement in Scotland* 8-17, John Minto *A history of the public library movement in Great Britain and Ireland* (LA, 1932) 25-33, and in Thomas Kelly's *Early public libraries* 113-114. Kirkwood is in the DNB. His tracts have been reprinted in full in John Cotton Dana and Henry W Kent *Literature of libraries in the seventeenth and eighteenth centuries,* and in part in John L Thornton *Selected readings in the history of librarianship* chapter 9. The *Overture* was reprinted as an appendix to Thomas Greenwood *Public libraries* (third edition, 1890).

ADDENDUM ON CATHEDRAL LIBRARIES
The study of the history of English cathedral libraries will be greatly facilitated by an excellent bibliography which was published too late to be mentioned earlier in this chapter: E Anne Read *A checklist of books, catalogues and periodical articles relating to the cathedral libraries of England* (Oxford Bibliographical Society, 1970). The purpose of this checklist is ' to provide as comprehensive a guide as possible to material concerning the cathedral libraries of England, from the later medieval period to the present day '.

CHAPTER SEVEN

SUBSCRIPTION LIBRARIES

One of the themes of library history is ' privilege '—the privilege of being literate enough to profit from books and the privilege of being wealthy enough to buy them, or borrow them from a subscription library.

In a wide sense, the term ' subscription library ' can be used to cover any type of library to which a subscription has to be paid, but in recent years it has been used mainly to refer to the private subscription libraries, and the commercial subscription libraries have been called circulating libraries.

Subscription and circulating libraries have an importance in library history which has not been sufficiently acknowledged, but thanks to the pioneering labours of Frank Beckwith, Dorothy Blakey, Hilda Hamlyn and Paul Kaufman, we now know something about their origins and early history, though a good deal of work remains to be done on the history of both types of library after 1800.

PRIVATE SUBSCRIPTION LIBRARIES

By the early eighteenth century, the reading public had grown large enough to create a demand for a much greater number of community libraries. When the century opened, the total library resources of the country were still very small. The gentry were able to pay for a library service and it was for them, especially, that the commercial circulating libraries were established. The gentry themselves founded private subscription libraries to provide books and periodicals of a scholarly kind.

The way towards the private subscription library was paved by the book club. A book club was a small society of friends, or neighbours, who subscribed to a common fund from which books were purchased for circulation. The normal method of operation was for the club to meet once a month to transact business.

Although many book clubs were established throughout the country, they had been overlooked by library historians until

Beckwith and Kaufman drew attention to them. We still have only a rough idea as to how many clubs were formed, as by their nature they were seldom mentioned in the contemporary newspapers and journals, and only a few records of individual clubs have come to light.

As far as we know, the first book clubs appeared in the 1730's, but they did not become numerous until the latter part of the eighteenth century. Although there were book clubs in towns, their special advantage was that they could thrive in small communities, where fully-fledged subscription libraries would have been impossible to establish. The membership of book clubs was middle-class and predominantly male, and the books purchased were serious, rather than recreational. Although a few of the clubs accumulated their books and thus became, in effect, subscription libraries, the majority sold the books to their own members.

The first subscription libraries appeared in Scotland. The earliest was a famous but untypical library, for its period, the library of the lead-miners of Leadhills, Lanarkshire, founded in 1741 (see Kaufman's *Libraries and their users* chapter XIV). Then came two gentlemen's subscription libraries, the Society Library at Dumfries (*c* 1745) and the Public Library at Kelso (1751).

The first private subscription library in England was established at Liverpool. 'In the year 1757, and probably for some time previously, a few gentlemen, residents of Liverpool, were accustomed to meet, for the discussion of literary subjects, at the house of Mr William Everard, a schoolmaster, in St Paul's Square. The reviews and other periodicals of the day were taken in, and read at their meetings; and by degrees a few other books were added . . . The success of this little society, and the benefit derived from the circulation of the books, suggested the desirableness of extending the plan; and in the beginning of the year 1758, several of the principal merchants, professional men, and tradesmen of the town, including probably all the members of the St Paul's Square Club . . . formed themselves into a society for establishing a circulating library' (extract from the preface to the *Catalogue of the Liverpool Library* (1850)). Thus, the first English subscription library was born out of a book club.

Over the next fifty years, subscription libraries were established in most of the larger towns, among them Leeds, Sheffield, Bristol, Bradford, Hull, Birmingham, Norwich, Leicester, Manchester and York. In a few towns a second library was established, but it seldom happened that both libraries prospered. Liverpool, which for many years had the Lyceum (as the first library came to be called) and the Athenaeum (1798), was a notable exception. At Leicester, Norwich, London and elsewhere, rivalry ended in amalgamation.

Private subscription libraries were promoted and supported largely by the middle classes, and in several towns the most active supporters, in the early days, were nonconformists.

The libraries were run by an elected committee, and the library ' laws ' or regulations could be remarkably comprehensive (see Charles Parish *History of the Birmingham Library* chapter V).

When, in due course, a paid librarian was appointed, he was the mere servant of the committee. His special responsibilities were to see that the regulations were enforced. It is worth noting that, even in these gentlemen's libraries, books were often damaged and stolen. The first librarians of the rate-supported public libraries had reason enough to insist that their stocks should be closed access.

Nevertheless, despite recurrent financial difficulties and occasional disputes over the committee's selection of books, the private subscription libraries usually managed to preserve the friendly atmosphere of a well conducted club. They were libraries where one could lounge, read, converse, hear a lecture and sometimes take refreshment. Kaufman is probably right when he says that these libraries had a snobbish appeal. But it is hardly likely that the founding members were actuated by snobbish motives, and it is clear that they were little interested in the provision of purely recreational literature, which most of these libraries were forced to provide in later years. In addition to books, newspapers and learned journals were purchased. The cost of the latter was a heavy charge on a library's income during the period when prices were inflated by stamp duty.

Many subscription libraries were proprietary libraries. To raise money for capital expenditure, each member of a proprietary library was obliged to purchase a ' share ' in the library, of which he then became a proprietor. As not every subscription library used this device to raise money, it is not strictly correct to refer to all subscription libraries as proprietary libraries.

Strangely, London had no permanent subscription library until the middle of the nineteenth century. The London Society Library (1785) and the Westminster Library (1789) were unable to survive, even after amalgamation, and in 1821 the books were sold.

The existing London Library was founded in 1841, largely through the efforts of Thomas Carlyle. Like many other scholars, Carlyle was frustrated at not being able to borrow the books he required. Unlike the earlier London subscription libraries, the new London Library was an immediate success. In 1845 it was moved to its present site in St James's Square and since then, by judicious purchases, augmented by numerous donations, it has built up an excellent stock of British and foreign works amounting to about 700,000 volumes.

The London Library has been well served both by its committee and its librarians. The modern development of the library owes much to Sir Charles Hagberg Wright (1862-1940). It was during his long period of office as librarian (1893-1940) that the present series of printed author and subject catalogues was inaugurated and the library was accorded the unusual distinction of the grant of a Royal Charter (1934).

The London Library differs from the provincial subscription libraries in several ways. It is not a proprietary library, with a limited membership, and it is not a local library—it has many ' country members '. Furthermore, whereas over the years the provincial libraries have found it necessary to buy (or rent from circulating libraries, such as Mudies and Harrods) popular recreational literature, the London Library has been able to adhere to its original intentions. It is still a library for scholars.

Since the latter part of the nineteenth century, the private subscription library has declined. The circulating libraries took away the weaker members and the developing city libraries some of the rest. In recent years, declining membership and severe increases in rates and other overheads have brought this type of library to the verge of extinction. A few of the provincial libraries remain —the Leeds Library (founded in 1768 and now the oldest survivor); the Portico Library, Manchester; the Bromley House Library, Nottingham; the Norfolk and Norwich Library, and Hull Subscription Library. The London Library, which was in grave financial straits a few years ago, has been preserved through the exertions of its committee. Recently it has been aided by the Arts Council.

The principal general sources of information on book clubs are the essays of Paul Kaufman, now available in his book *Libraries and their users* (LA, 1969) chapters III and IV. For an excellent account of an individual club see John Morley ' Newark Book Society 1777-1872 ' *Library history* 1 (3) Spring 1968 77-86.

There is no comprehensive history of private subscription libraries. Their early history has been surveyed in Frank Beckwith ' The eighteenth century proprietary library in England ' *Journal of documentation* 3 (2) September 1947 81-98, Paul Kaufman *Libraries and their users* chapter XVI (but see, if possible, the original text ' The community library ' *Transactions of the American Philosophical Society* new series 57 (7) October 1967 25-38 and appendices), and Thomas Kelly's *Early public libraries* chapter VI.

Detailed histories of individual subscription libraries are few. The best example is *The Leeds Library 1768-1968* (Leeds Library, 1968). Although no author's name appears on the title-page, this history is undoubtedly the work of Frank Beckwith, until recently librarian of the Leeds Library. Charles Parish *History of the Birmingham Library* (LA, 1966) is mainly concerned with the early history of the library, from 1779 to 1799. The later years are dealt with all too briefly. In 1955, Birmingham Library was merged with the Birmingham and Midland Institute. John Russell *A history of the Nottingham Subscription Library* (1916) is little more than an outline history of an interesting library which was founded in 1816.

All that is known about the early and unsuccessful London subscription libraries will be found in Kaufman's *Libraries and their users* chapter I. There is no detailed history of the present London Library. Outline histories will be found in Stanley Gillam 'The London Library' *The library world* LXI (717) March 1960 180-184, and the same author's '125 years of the London Library' in Robert L Collison (*ed*) *Progress in library science 1966* (Butterworths, 1966) chapter 14. Sir Charles Hagberg Wright is in the DNB. See also Stanley Gillam 'Hagberg Wright and the London Library' *Library history* 1 (1) Spring 1967 24-27. The one part of the London Library's history which has been dealt with at length is the story of its origins. This will be found in Simon Nowell-Smith ' Carlyle and the London Library ', *English libraries 1800-1850* (H K Lewis, 1958) 59-78.

The post-war difficulties of the remaining private subscription libraries are discussed in Geoffrey Whatmore 'Subscription libraries and the cost of living' *Library review* XVI (123) Autumn 1957 162-165.

CIRCULATING LIBRARIES

The history of the commercial circulating libraries remains largely untold. Its outline can be traced fairly accurately, but much of the detail has either been lost, or else lies buried in the archives of the firms concerned. The librarians of non-commercial libraries have shewn little interest in circulating libraries, except that for many years they were only too willing to buy their discarded books. Edward Edwards was well aware of the existence of circulating libraries, but he did not write about them and, as Dr Munford points out, he 'effectively deflected the attention of the Select Committee of 1849 ' from them. At one time Edwards was a subscriber to Mudie's Select Library (indeed he claimed to be Mudie's first subscriber) and in building up the stock of Manchester public library he bought extensively from Mudie's ex-circulating stock (W A Munford *Edward Edwards 1812-1886* (LA, 1963), 95, 211).

The notion that circulating libraries, from first to last, were concerned only with popular fiction dies hard. It is true that most of their subscribers wanted little else from them, but circulating libraries varied a great deal in size and quality and some of them provided many serious works. In recent years, a few library historians have been at pains to trace the surviving copies of the printed catalogues of circulating libraries. Unfortunately, these catalogues can only be used effectively in association with circulation records and these are rarely found. Nevertheless, where the catalogues shew that serious books were stocked it is reasonable to assume that there was some demand for them.

It has often been stated that the history of the circulating library begins in the year 1726, or thereabouts, when Allan Ramsay (1686-1758), poet and bookseller, opened a library at Edinburgh, but the origins of the circulating library are not, in fact, so precise and go back further in time. It is now known that, in the seventeenth century, several London booksellers hired out part of their stocks to their customers. But the circulating library as a regular enterprise belongs to the eighteenth century and its growth was undoubtedly stimulated by the rising popularity of the novel. By the 1750's, there were circulating libraries in London and the larger provincial towns and they had become a necessary amenity of the new spas and watering places.

The period between Smollett and Scott gave birth to the Gothic novel of sensation and sentimentality. Novels of this type were the speciality of a publishing house called the Minerva Press, owned by William Lane (1745-1814). Lane not only published the type of books which many circulating library subscribers preferred, but from about 1770 he operated a circulating library of his own in London, the Minerva Library. Furthermore, he encouraged shopkeepers throughout the country to operate circulating libraries by selling them suitable collections of books and providing them with instructions on library procedure.

The methods used by the eighteenth century circulating libraries were basically the same as those used by their modern successors. Subscriptions were nicely graded, so that those who paid the most got the best service, and books could be borrowed casually against a deposit, as well as by subscription.

In the full version of his essay ' The community library ', Kaufman includes a section called ' Contemporary reactions to circulating libraries '. This shows that the early circulating libraries were heartily condemned by the righteous, with little justification.

When the nineteenth century opened, books were expensive and they remained so for many years. For the greater part of the century, many novels were first published in three volumes (called ' three deckers ') at 10s 6d a volume. The three decker was in the ascendant when Mudie's Select Library was established and it helped it to prosper. This famous Victorian institution was founded in 1842 by a bookseller called Charles Edward Mudie (1818-1890). The library soon became popular, and within a few years it was removed from Southampton Row to larger premises in New Oxford Street.

Mudie's success was due to extensive advertising, the provision of popular new books in large numbers, a cheap basic subscription (one guinea) and the exclusion of all books of doubtful moral value. The library was quite deliberately called ' Select ' and Mudie made it known that the selection of books was done with scrupulous care.

The library was well organised. It had its own delivery service in London. It had a ' country department ', which despatched boxes of books to private and institutional members at home and overseas. The stock was enormous and went a good way beyond the popular novel. Latterly it included a foreign language section. There were other large circulating libraries in the nineteenth century, but none to compare with Mudie's. It was the favourite library of the ' carriage class '.

Mudie's had only two or three branches, but as books from Mudie's were rented by clubs, private subscription libraries and small circulating libraries all over the country, its fame was nation-wide.

I have heard that Mudie's archives were destroyed during the second world war, but we know enough about it from contemporary references to appreciate why it was so highly esteemed and why it declined after its founder died. In the excellent description of the library by William C Preston, published in 1894, there is a reference to the many thousands of discarded books in the basement. ' Some of them made a sensation in their time. The great librarian had to purchase thousands of them to meet the eager demand of his readers; but nobody asks for them now—and, worse still, nobody will buy them'. When this was written, the three decker had been killed by the book trade, and Mudie's never managed to adjust itself to a changed world, where new books were cheap enough for the gentry to buy, or easier to borrow from the branch of a chain circulating library close at hand.

Railway travel was a great encouragement to reading. The need for good railway bookstalls was met by W H Smith & Son. Under the energetic direction of William Henry Smith the younger (1825-1891), the firm obtained a near monopoly of railway bookstalls. When Smith decided to add circulating libraries to them, he invited Mudie to join forces with him. Mudie refused and in 1860 Smith's started a chain of libraries out of their own resources.

Smith, like Mudie, was a man of high principles. Between them these two men did much to raise the reputation of the circulating library, which in Lane's day had been called 'the source of all the vices and follies of mankind'. But the power which they exercised in the book world was a mixed blessing, and several writers resented having to emasculate their novels to prevent them from being rejected by Mudie and Smith.

When the present century opened, Mudie's and Smith's were faced with competition from an efficient chain of shop libraries operated by Boots. Boots began to add libraries to their chemist shops in 1900, at the suggestion of the wife of Jesse Boot, the founder of the firm. Under the direction of a librarian appointed from Mudie's, Boots' Booklovers' Libraries were rapidly established throughout the country. In 1906, having lost some of their railway contracts, Smith's opened a number of bookshops to which they transferred their libraries. Eventually, Boots and Smith's together owned about 1,000 libraries. The libraries of the two firms were very much alike. The subscriptions were low, the books clean, the regulations simple, and readers could exchange their books at any branch.

The early years of the present century also saw the establishment of several more good quality circulating libraries similar to Mudie's. The Times Book Club was established in 1905 and Harrods Library in 1914.

By this time, there were circulating libraries for all but the poorer members of the community. In the larger towns there had been a few shabby circulating libraries for the working class for some years, but in the 1930's chains of ' tuppenny libraries ' were established throughout the country. The advent of these cheap circulating libraries, which affected the fiction issnes of public libraries, provoked several articles in our professional journals which make curious reading today.

When the demand for circulating libraries was at its peak, Mudie's went bankrupt. After Mudie's death, in 1890, the fortunes of the firm had steadily declined. The library was closed by court order in July 1937. The other libraries flourished until the 1950's, when there was a rapid loss of subscribers, for which television, paperback books and the improved service offered by public libraries were held to blame. Day's Library, which claimed to have been founded in 1740, closed in 1957 and the Times Book Club in 1962. This left only one notable circulating library in London, Harrods Library, which still survives. Of much greater significance was the closure of the two national chains of circulating libraries. Smith's libraries were closed in 1961 and Boots' libraries in 1966.

It was never easy to make money out of circulating libraries, and profits always depended upon the sale of discarded volumes. Most of the twentieth century libraries were subsidised out of general sales, because they encouraged regular visits to the shops and stores which housed them. But even in their humblest form they are part of our social history and should not be neglected. In recent years a few library historians have turned their attention to them and it is to be hoped that the work they have done will encourage further research.

The study of circulating library history presents many difficulties. Kaufman has recently given us a useful history of the early years, but the story after 1800 has to be pieced together from a variety of sources. J G Ollé ' The lost libraries ' *Library review*

20 (7) Autumn 1966 452-456 is a brief, informal history, inspired by the closure of Boots' libraries.

On the eighteenth century see Paul Kaufman *Libraries and their users* (LA, 1969) chapters XVI and XVII and Paul Kaufman ' The community library' *Transactions of the American Philosophical Society* new series 57 (7) October 1967 6-25 and appendices, and H M Hamlyn ' Eighteenth century circulating libraries in England' *Library* 5th series 1 (3) December 1946 197-222. The principal source of information on William Lane (who is not in the DNB) is Dorothy Blakey *The Minerva Press 1790-1820* (Bibliographical Society, 1939).

The best account of Mudie's Select Library is G L Griest 'A Victorian Leviathan' *Nineteenth-century fiction* 20 (2) September 1965 103-126. Other sources of information include R A Colby ' The librarian rules the roost' *Wilson library bulletin* 26 (8) April 1952 623-627, and Amy Cruse *The Victorians and their books* (Allen & Unwin, 1935) chapter XV. The contemporary description of Mudie's, referred to above, is William C Preston *Mudie's Library* (1894), a pamphlet reprint of an article published in *Good words* October 1894.

There is no adequate account of Smith's libraries, but see R A Colby ' That he who rides may read' *Wilson library bulletin* 27 (4) December 1952 300-306 and Viscount Chilston *W H Smith* (Routledge, 1965) 44-45.

On Boots' libraries see ' Boots, stock and branch' *Times literary supplement* February 3rd 1966 92. On the cheap circulating libraries and their impact on public libraries see T E Callander ' The twopenny library' *Library Association record* 3rd series III (3) March 1933 88-90.

Useful information on the state of the circulating libraries before the last war will be found in F D Sanders *(ed) British book trade organisation* (Allen & Unwin, 1939) 133-147. On the decline of circulating libraries see John Hampden *The book world today* (Allen & Unwin, 1957) chapter 17 and R L Collison *Progress in library science 1965* (Butterworths, 1965) chapter 14.

CHAPTER EIGHT

THE MECHANICS' INSTITUTES

The libraries of the mechanics' institutes are difficult to classify. Although they were available only on payment of a subscription, it would be incorrect to describe them as subscription libraries, partly because they were institutional libraries and partly because they were usually subsidised, directly or indirectly, by the gentry. Kelly suggests that they should be grouped, with the working men's libraries and Samuel Brown's itinerating libraries, under the heading ' philanthropic libraries ' (*Early public libraries* 243).

The major difficulty we encounter when studying the history of the MI libraries is that there is no definitive history of the MI movement. The best general history, which forms part of Thomas Kelly's biography of George Birkbeck, is largely confined to the early years of the movement. As Dr Kelly explains, for the period after 1851 the materials for writing a general history are scanty; there are no contemporary national surveys and very few histories of individual institutes to draw upon. One thing is clear, however. The MIs did not fade away as soon as the first Public Libraries Acts were passed. On the contrary, they increased in numbers for at least another ten years.

It is difficult to say when the MI movement reached its peak. Kelly says ' as far as one can judge the peak of the movement was not reached until about 1860 ' and that the institutes were ' still vigorous ' in 1875 (Thomas Kelly *A history of adult education in Great Britain* 198-199).

The origins of the MI movement can be traced back to the eighteenth century, but the first institute proper was the Edinburgh School of Arts (1821). The Glasgow Mechanics' Institute (1823) is of greater importance, however, as the publicity it received led to the foundation of MIs in other towns. A few months before the Glasgow MI was established, the *Mechanics' magazine* was founded. When the editor heard of the Glasgow institute, he started a campaign to found a similar institute in London. There was a quick response and the London MI was established in 1824, with George Birkbeck as its first president.

George Birkbeck (1776-1841) has frequently been called the founder of the MI movement, but this requires explanation. At the beginning of the nineteenth century, Birkbeck organised classes for artisans at the Anderson Institute in Glasgow, but he left Glasgow in 1804, and when the artisans broke away from the Anderson Institute to found their own, Birkbeck was working in London. All the same, his role in the history of the MI movement is important. From 1824 until he died, in 1841, Birkbeck was a staunch patron of the MI movement and his work for the London MI alone is worthy of remembrance.

Despite setbacks due to periods of trade depression, the movement progressed rapidly. By 1850, there were over 600 institutes. How many were established altogether it is hard to say. Not all MIS actually called themselves MIS.

The decline of the institutes was slow at first, but it accelerated rapidly during the last twenty years of the century. As many of the institutes had only one successful feature, their library, the adoption of the Public Libraries Acts by the local authority was often the signal for the local MI to close.

The MI libraries were originally intended to support the educational work of the institutes, but through lack of competent lecturers and undue optimism as to the potential demand for formal instruction, the classes often faded away within a few years. Although the libraries survived, they did so only by adding to their stocks recreational literature. J F C Harrison says that, by the 1840's, 'the emphasis in most of the institutes had shifted completely to literary or fashionable topics, both in the lectures and choice of books for the library' (*Learning and living* 1790-1960 (Routledge, 1961) 67-68). Faced with increasing demands for the provision of fiction, newspapers and the more popular periodicals, the managers of the mechanics' institutes were obliged to make some concessions for fear of losing subscribers.

In the early years of the movement, the stocks of the MI libraries were very small and based too much on donations, but the institutes which managed to survive the difficult pioneering period were able to improve their library stocks by the addition of requested books purchased from income.

The library of a MI could sometimes be used by paying a library subscription only, but more often it was necessary to become a full member of the institute. The subscriptions varied, but most of them were small. A full subscription was sometimes as low as a shilling a quarter, but when members were sick, or unemployed, even the smallest subscriptions were more than they could afford.

In assessing the value of the MI libraries, it must be remembered that most of them were very small and that there was a very great difference between the best and the worst. Even the best of them did not encourage study very much, but they did encourage reading. The most successful MI libraries were those in the larger towns, especially those in the midlands and the north. The institutes of the railway towns such as Crewe, Derby and Swindon, had long and useful lives, thanks partly to financial support from the railway companies. An institute thrived only if it was well supported and well managed. The Leicester MI gave up the struggle for survival in 1871. The Nottingham MI was successful from its early days and still survives. At the beginning of this century its library was one of the best in the county.

In their heyday, the large MI libraries were in many ways similar to public libraries. They had lending departments (usually closed-access), reference collections and large reading rooms. They were open from ten to twelve hours a day and they were administered by full-time salaried librarians. (Dr Ernest Baker, who eventually became the first director of the school of librarianship at University College, London, was at one time librarian of the Midland Railway Institute at Derby.)

In several parts of the country, unions of MIS were established. One of these, the Yorkshire Union, won for itself a unique place in library history. In 1852, James Hole, the energetic honorary secretary of the Union, initiated a village library scheme to bring some of the benefits of adult education to those areas of Yorkshire where MIS could not be established. The Yorkshire village libraries continued to operate until the 1920's, when they were replaced by county library centres.

64

Against these successes one must set the many failures. Overall, the greatest failure of the MIS and their libraries was that they were unable to recruit, or retain in membership, the unskilled workers. In some institutes, certainly not in all, the majority of the members were clerks, shopkeepers, teachers and clergymen.

There is a great deal we do not know, and may never know, about the libraries of the MIS. Such information as we have must be used with caution. The evidence on these libraries submitted to the Ewart Committee is of great interest, but it is, of course, a statement of the position in 1849, when the MI movement was still young.

The literature on the MI libraries, as distinct from that on the MI movement generally, is slender. The essay ' Mechanics' institutes and public libraries ' by Joan Edmondson, published as an appendix to W A Munford *Penny rate* (LA, 1951), is still worth reading, but it needs revision in the light of later research. The same observation applies to the section on the MIS and their libraries in Richard D Altick *The English common reader* (University of Chicago Press, 1957) chapter 9. There is no satisfactory account of the MI libraries in their later years, but for the period up to 1850 see Thomas Kelly's *Early public libraries* 228-237 and ' George Birkbeck and Mechanics' Institutes ' by W A Munford in *English libraries 1800-1850* (H K Lewis, 1958) 33-58.

There are scattered but useful references to MI libraries in Thomas Kelly *George Birkbeck* (Liverpool University Press, 1957) and Mabel Tylecote *The mechanics' institutes of Lancashire and Yorkshire before 1851* (Manchester University Press, 1957). On the decay of the MI libraries see Thomas Greenwood *Public libraries* (Cassell, fourth edition, 1891) 32. For a detailed account of an outstandingly successful MI library see P Cropper ' The library of the Nottingham Mechanics' Institution ' *Library* IV (2) 1892 45-49.

On the Yorkshire Village Library (as the scheme was called) see Joseph Daykin ' Village libraries ' *Library Association record* IX 1907 367-371 and J F C Harrison *Social reform in Victorian Leeds: the work of James Hole* (Leeds, Thoresby Society, 1954) 39-41.

The best source of information on the MI movement at large is the history by Kelly which forms book two of his biography of Birkbeck. For a shorter account see Thomas Kelly *A history of adult education in Great Britain* (Liverpool University Press, 1962) and John Thomas Lea *The history and development of the Mechanics' Institutions* (Oldham, Research in Librarianship, 1968), a pamphlet based on an essay submitted to the LA in 1949.

Two important contemporary works on the mechanics' institutes which have been difficult to obtain for many years have recently been reprinted: J W Hudson *The history of adult education* (1851; reprinted Woburn Press, 1970) and James Hole *An essay on the history and management of literary, scientific and mechanics' institutions* (1853; reprinted Frank Cass, 1970).

The MI movement spread overseas. It was particularly successful in Australia, where MIs flourished until the 1890's, with the help of government grants. See J Balnaves *Australian libraries* (Bingley, 1966) 16-18.

(*Early public libraries* 90). A particularly interesting example of an endowed library in a small community is the Plume Library at Maldon, Essex, founded by the Rev Thomas Plume in 1704, which still survives.

Information concerning the endowed libraries of Scotland is scanty, with two interesting exceptions, the libraries of Dundee and Innerpeffray. In 1636, a library at Dundee which had come into existence towards the end of the previous century passed from parochial into municipal control and had a useful life as a lending library until it was destroyed by fire, in 1841. The isolated library at Innerpeffray, in Perthshire, which still survives, is one of the most interesting endowed libraries of which we have any knowledge. It came into being early in the eighteenth century and although it was intended ' for the benefit and encouragement of young students ', it was used as a public lending library by people from a variety of professions and occupations. Although a smaller library than Chetham's, and serving a very much smaller community, the Innerpeffray library was used more effectively than Chetham's.

The history of the early endowed libraries is so complicated that students are advised to read the relevant sections in Kelly's pamphlet, *Public libraries in Great Britain before 1850* and Paul Kaufman ' The community library ' *Transactions of the American Philosophical Society* new series 57 (7) October 1967 38-45 before reading *Early public libraries* chapters IV and V.

On the individual endowed libraries mentioned above, see the following additional sources of information:

Chetham's Library: Hilda Lofthouse ' Chetham's Library ' *Book collector* 5 (4) Winter 1956 323-330, H S A Smith ' Readers and books in a seventeenth century library ' *Library Association record* 65 (10) October 1963 366-369, Edward Edwards *Memoirs of libraries* vol I 623-679 and *Chetham's Hospital and Library* (Chetham's Hospital, 1956).

Bristol Library: Geoffrey Langley 'A place to put bookes ' *Library Association record* 65 (11) November 1963 397-402.

Ipswich Library: 'An ancient library ' *Times literary supplement* August 18 1950 524.

Norwich Library: G A Stephen *Three centuries of a city library* (Norwich Public Libraries, 1917) and Philip Hepworth and Mary Alexander *City of Norwich libraries: history and treasures* (Norwich Public Libraries, 1957).

Leicester Library: This library has been written about surprisingly little. The best source of information is a locally published pamphlet: Frank S Herne *History of the Town Library and of the Permanent Library, Leicester* (Leicester, 1891).

Plume Library, Maldon: Catalogue of the Plume Library at Maldon, Essex compiled by S G Deed (Maldon, Plume Library Trustees, 1959). See the foreword by Sir Frank Francis.

Innerpeffray Library: Paul Kaufman *Libraries and their users* (LA, 1969) chapter XIII, which provides further references.

Dundee Library: Kaufman's *Libraries and their users* chapter XII, but do not overlook the special note on this library in Kelly's *Early public libraries* 87-88.

ITINERATING LIBRARIES

Until the railway age, many readers who lived in rural areas had to be content with very few books. Something was done, but not nearly enough, to provide the clergy with books and from the eighteenth century some villages had book clubs, but they were for the gentry, for the most part.

The early nineteenth century saw the introduction, in Scotland, of a system of ' itinerating libraries ' which seemed highly promising, at the time it was under the direction of its sponsor.

This type of library provision was devised and initially administered by Samuel Brown (1779-1839), merchant and Provost of Haddington, East Lothian, a thinly populated county on the Firth of Forth. Ambitious to found instructive libraries where none existed, Brown considered how a little money might be used to the greatest advantage. Realising that a library soon outlives its usefulness if the stock remains static (a common defect of the parochial and early town libraries), Brown hit upon the notion of establishing a number of small libraries, with differing stocks, and moving the collections around every two years. Four ' libraries' of fifty volumes each were sent to East Lothian villages in 1817, where they were placed under the control of honorary librarians. The exchange of books after an interval of two years was so successful in sustaining interest that Brown was encouraged to extend his scheme throughout the rest of the county. To raise money for this purpose, Brown secured annual donations from the gentry by giving them the exclusive privilege of borrowing books when they were new.

There were eventually fifty itinerating libraries in East Lothian, but after Brown's death they gradually faded away, through lack of an energetic director to succeed him. Furthermore, the public became tired of the moral and religious literature which formed the greater part of the stock, and issues declined when Brown was forced to levy a charge of 1d per volume when books were borrowed during their first year at each village centre.

Brown's son, the Rev John Croumbie Brown, told the Ewart Committee, in 1849, that only twenty libraries remained and that their use was declining.

Although Brown's scheme was much praised (by Lord Brougham and Samuel Smiles, among others), he could never obtain enough money to support it. The scheme was copied in several other Scottish counties, but nowhere with lasting success. The itinerating libraries sponsored by the Yorkshire Union of Mechanics' Institutes were in use for many years, as I have previously mentioned, but they were better organised and more securely financed.

The best introduction to Brown's libraries is L G Durbidge ' Pioneer itinerator ' *Times literary supplement* March 6 1969 246. There is also an excellent account of them in W R Aitken *History of the public library movement in Scotland* (1964) 40-53. For the evidence submitted to the Ewart Committee see the *Ewart report* (1849) 73-79. The primary source of information on Brown (who is not in the DNB) is the privately printed memoir by his son: Samuel Brown *Some account of itinerating libraries and their founder* (1856). An extract from this is included in Thornton's *Selected readings* chapter 12.

We have now considered all the major types of community libraries which existed before the rate-supported public library appeared.

The first historian of the public library movement was Edward Edwards, who chronicled the early years in his *Memoirs of libraries* (1859) and in *Free town libraries* (1869). The first long range history was John J Ogle *The free library: its history and present condition* (George Allen 1897). This is not a satisfactory history, but it includes information on adoptions, rejections and library benefactors which is still of interest.

John Minto *A history of the public library movement in Great Britain and Ireland* (Allen & Unwin, 1932) is largely a legislative history. As such, it remains of value. It includes a lengthy summary of the *Ewart report,* a ' Conspectus of the various Acts of Parliament' (by James Hutt) and a biographical dictionary of ' prominent workers and benefactors '.

The full history of the public library movement in Great Britain is now being written by Dr Thomas Kelly, but even when it is available there is likely to be continuing need for the readable and helpful outline history by W A Munford, *Penny rate* (LA, 1951). Although a shorter history than Minto's, *Penny rate* takes a much broader view of public library development. In the limited space at his disposal, Dr Munford wisely abandoned a strict chronological arrangement. Instead, he deals separately with various important aspects of public library history.

The first part of James Howard Wellard *Book selection* (Grafton, 1937) is a pioneer attempt to determine the ' social objectives' of the public library at various periods of its history, but this is done more successfully in W J Murison *The public library* (Harrap, 1955). See also Dr Kelly's tentative conclusions in Thomas Kelly ' Public libraries and public opinion' *Library Association record* 68 (7) July 1966 246-251.

It is impossible to discuss the history of the public library movement without making constant references to the classic reports on public libraries. These reports are usually referred to by the names of their authors, or by the names of the chairmen of the investigating committees. I have therefore provided below, for ease of reference, a chronological list of these reports, showing both their official titles and the names by which they are commonly known:

Ewart report (1849): Report from the Select Committee on public libraries, together with the proceedings of the committee, minutes of evidence and appendix (1849). Reprinted by Frank Cass (1968) and Irish University Press (1968). Chairman: William Ewart MP.

Ewart report (1850): Report from the Select Committee on public libraries, together with the proceedings of the committee, minutes of evidence, appendix, and index (1850). Reprinted Irish University Press (1968). Chairman: William Ewart MP.

Adams report (1915): W G S Adams *A report on library provision and policy* (CUKT, 1915).

Ministry of Reconstruction's report (1919): Ministry of Reconstruction. *Third interim report of the Adult Education Committee: libraries and museums* (HMSO, 1919).

Mitchell report (1924): J M Mitchell *The public library system of Great Britain and Ireland 1921-1923* (CUKT, 1924).

Kenyon report (1927): Board of Education. Public Libraries Committee. *Report on public libraries in England and Wales* (HMSO, 1927). Chairman: Sir Frederic Kenyon.

McColvin report (1942): Lionel R McColvin *The public library system of Great Britain* (LA, 1942).

Roberts report (1959): Ministry of Education. *The structure of the public library service in England and Wales* (HMSO, 1959). Chairman: Sir Sydney Roberts.

Bourdillon report (1962): Ministry of Education. *Standards of public library service in England and Wales* (HMSO, 1962).

The advent of the rate-supported public library is one of the best-known events in British library history, but certain features of it are worth emphasising. In the first place, it is extraordinary how much was done by Edward Edwards, a man of humble origins and modest status. Secondly, bearing in mind the state

73

3*

of the country at the time and the urgent need for government action on vital matters such as education and public health, it is remarkable that the Public Libraries Act reached the statute book at all, and in such a short space of time.

Edward Edwards (1812-1886) was the son of a builder. We know too little of his youth, but it is fairly certain that his formal education was small and that he educated himself, to a large extent, by reading. How he came to the notice of William Ewart, MP for Dumfries Burghs, and how Ewart brought about the appointment of a Select Committee to consider ' the best means of extending the establishment of libraries freely open to the public, especially in large towns in Great Britain and Ireland ' need not be explained here as the details will be found in *Penny rate*. Ewart was zealously supported by Joseph Brotherton, MP for Salford (see J S Cowan ' Joseph Brotherton and the public library movement' *Library Association record* 59 (5) May 1957 156-159). The evidence appended to the *Ewart report* seems to present a complete picture of British libraries at the middle of the nineteenth century. In fact, it does not. The committee was not interested (perhaps one should say that Ewart and Edwards were not interested) in subscription libraries for the gentry; it was, however, very much interested in cathedral, parochial and town libraries, the libraries of the mechanics' institutes, itinerating libraries, the British Museum Library and the other copyright libraries. Unfortunately, the committee set to work so quickly that the witnesses had little time to prepare their evidence and this was particularly hard on Edward Edwards, who was required to answer hundreds of questions about libraries at home and abroad.

We now know, through the work of Dr Kelly and other recent investigators, that the committee did not always have the full facts. It would probably have made no difference anyway. The parochial and MI libraries which were not listed in the evidence were as unsatisfactory as those that were.

The committee recommended that 'A power be given by Parliament enabling Town Councils to levy a small rate for the creation and support of Town Libraries '.

'Judged by any reasonable standards', says Munford, 'the Act of 1850 is not an impressive document'. But note, also, Murison's observation: 'The 1850 Act was passed despite lack of proof that the public libraries were wanted. That they were needed is a different matter ' (*The public library* 24).

Two discouraging features of the 1850 Act were removed in 1855, when a further Act gave permission to buy books and raised the rate limitation from $\frac{1}{2}d$ to 1d. The 1d rate lasted in England and Wales until 1919, except where local authorities obtain exemption from it through local Acts. About sixty of the larger authorities took action to raise the library rate. According to Savage, it was not difficult to obtain Parliamentary sanction.

The chronological table of adoptions in the *Kenyon report* (1927) 235-239 and the graph in J H Wellard's *Book selection* 34 show that local authorities were in no hurry to adopt the Acts. Many of the campaigners for adoption, in the early years, stressed the particular benefits of public libraries for the working classes. It was seriously argued that public libraries would counteract drunkenness and crime, and the well-known frontispiece to the first edition of Thomas Greenwood's *Free public libraries* was not intended to amuse.

Thomas Greenwood (1851-1908) was an untiring supporter of the public library movement. As a young man he had used the Manchester Public Library and later he became, for a short while, a branch librarian at Sheffield. When he became a successful publisher, he took it upon himself to stimulate adoptions of the Public Libraries Acts far and wide. In this cause he travelled widely, distributed circulars and answered countless queries. In 1886, he published the first edition of his useful manual *Free public libraries*, which James Duff Brown, who helped Greenwood to revise the later editions, called ' The Bible of the movement'. Brown had a great admiration for Greenwood—much more than he had for Carnegie. ' It is not overstating the case ', he said, ' to say that, for hard, disinterested and fruitful service on behalf of libraries in Britain, his record is unapproached even by Edward Edwards or William Ewart '.

Greenwood is in the DNB, but the best appreciation of his work is the anonymous article (undoubtedly by Brown) 'Thomas Greenwood' *The library world* 1 (7) January 1899 116-121. See also Thornton's *Selected readings* chapter 31. There is a full biography of Greenwood, Grace Carlton *Spadework: the story of Thomas Greenwood* (Hutchinson, 1949), but it is not sufficiently informative on his library activities and it is poorly documented.

Greenwood's own publications, which are a useful quarry of information on the progress of the public library movement up to the end of the century, are as follows: *Free public libraries* (1886, second edition 1887), then with change of title *Public libraries* (third edition 1890, fourth edition 1891); *Greenwood's library year book* (1897) and *The British library year book* (1900).

Thomas Kelly says that up to about 1886 'the main emphasis among the promoters of libraries was social and philanthropic rather than cultural, and that the libraries were generally regarded as a means towards the improvement of the working classes'. After 1886, there was increasing emphasis on the educational value of public libraries, which then became 'more respectable'.

It was during the 1880's that adoptions of the Acts began to accelerate. The boom period was from 1890 to 1910. This was partly, but by no means altogether, due to the benefactions of Andrew Carnegie.

From their early days, public library authorities relied upon benefactors to provide money, books, sites and especially buildings. In some towns there was one particular benefactor: in others a 'subscription list' was opened. (See *Penny rate* chapter VI.) Ogle calculated that the list of local benefactors he compiled for the period 1888 to 1896 represented 'a value exceeding half a million' (*The free library* 67-70).

In the preface to his fascinating album of photographs of public libraries at the end of the century, *Views and memoranda of public libraries* (1901), Alfred Cotgreave pays special tribute to John Passmore Edwards (1823-1911) 'for his princely generosity in founding libraries'. Within a few years, however, Passmore Edwards had been eclipsed as a library benefactor by Andrew Carnegie (1835-1919).

Carnegie gave away, personally, nearly £2 million for public library buildings in the UK, most of it during the period 1900-1912. The majority of his individual gifts (although not the greater part of his money) was given to small authorities to encourage them to adopt the Acts. Brown and a few other librarians were highly critical of Carnegie's policy from the beginning of his operations. He gave money for buildings only, not for sites or for books. Dr Adams accounted for 366 library buildings paid for, in whole or in part, by Carnegie. They were spread over 292 authorities.

Carnegie's policy was simple and, on the face of it, sound. He wanted to encourage local communities to help themselves. Unfortunately, his programme of library aid became the victim of the flaws in our library legislation and of his own pride.

In 1913, Carnegie handed over his library responsibilities to the Carnegie United Kingdom Trust. It would have been better for his reputation as a library benefactor had he established the CUKT earlier. In 1914, the trustees invited Dr W G S Adams to report on the public library situation, with special reference to Carnegie's benefactions. The *Adams report* was published in 1915. It is a most important document, as it influenced the CUKT's own policy. It also harmed Carnegie's reputation as a personal library benefactor, with its criticisms of ' over-building '. In the long run Carnegie's buildings served a useful purpose; at the time they were given, however, many authorities could not afford to stock them with books.

On Carnegie's benefactions see the *Adams report*, J G Ollé 'Andrew Carnegie: the unloved benefactor' *The library world* LXX (826) April 1969 255-262 and R C Benge ' Life without father: the post-Carnegie period' *Library Association record* 59 (2) February 1957 49-52.

The public library movement made slow progress in London until the end of the century (see Greenwood's *Public libraries* (1891) chapter XVI). This was partly due to the peculiarities of its local government, and partly to the opposition of militant ratepayer's associations. Several London parishes (there were no metropolitan boroughs until 1899) delayed adopting the Acts for many years. Marylebone, which rejected Carnegie's money, was one. St Pancras was another. Usually, once a public library service had been provided, the opposition died away, even although it did not entirely disappear. St Pancras, which accepted Carnegie's offer of £40,000, later changed its mind. It is an interesting example of a public library service falling victim to party politics. See J G Ollé ' Prayers at Highgate ' *Library review* 21 (7) Autumn 1968 351-356.

The early public libraries obtained their chief librarians where they could. The larger towns, which offered the better salaries, were often fortunate enough to obtain chiefs with some library experience, if only as librarian of a circulating library, or the library of a mechanics' institute. At the end of the century, James Duff Brown made an interesting analysis of chief librarians and discovered that many of them had been trained at the large city libraries, such as Birmingham. (See J D Brown ' Where do we get out librarians?' *The library world* III (29) November 1900 124-127.)

The penny rate period produced more capable librarians than one might expect, in view of the modest salaries and the aggravating conditions of work, among them Edwards, John Potter Briscoe, John James Ogle, John Ballinger and James Duff Brown.

Edward Edwards' short term of office as librarian of Manchester was not only important in the development of the Manchester library. The work he did there was closely observed and copied in other libraries. After his dismissal from Manchester, Edwards' contact with the public library movement was mainly through his publications. He died in 1886, by which time the public library service was really beginning to develop. Thomas Greenwood *Edward Edwards* (Scott, Greenwood, 1902) was a labour of love, but it is a rather dull biography and incomplete. It has now been superseded by W A Munford *Edward Edwards 1812-1886: portrait of a librarian* (LA, 1963). There is a good short account of Edwards in the DNB.

Edwards was the outstanding librarian at the beginning of the rate restriction period; James Duff Brown was the greatest librarian at the end of it. It is not easy, today, to explain Brown's importance in public library history. He did not administer a great library. Open access would have come without him. His text-books and his classification schemes have had their day. But when he died, the LA devoted a large part of the *Library association record* to his obituary notices. The essential point about Brown is that his faith and enthusiasm inspired faith in others. It should be noted, however, that in the paper he wrote on the British library scene in 1912 (printed for the first time in Dr Munford's biography) he seems to have lost his own faith in public library progress.

At long last we have a biography of Brown, short but readable, and amply illustrated with quotations from his own writings: W A Munford *James Duff Brown: 1862-1914* (LA, 1968). See also Ernest A Savage ' James Duff Brown after fifty years ' *Library review* XVII (135) Autumn 1960 489-495, and the obituary notices in the *Library Association record* 16 May 1914 239-263.

During the first world war, the public library service suffered from loss of staff and reduced income. The government, far from commending the use of public libraries, encouraged local authorities to economise on them. It was during the war, however, that the CUKT made several experiments to discover the best way to run a rural library service. (See F A Keyse ' The birth of county libraries: CUKT experiments 1915-1919 ' *Journal of librarianship* 1 (3) July 1969 183-190.)

In 1919, a group of London librarians, led by George Roebuck and assisted by John Ballinger and the CUKT, successfully campaigned for a new Public Libraries Act. (See Ernest A Savage ' George Roebuck and the rate limit ' *The library world* LV (646) April 1954 167-171.) The 1919 Act (England and Wales) removed parliamentary rate restriction and gave library powers to the county councils.

The LA's interest in public libraries is shown by the several references to them in its charter, but without a full history of the LA it is difficult to assess its work for the public library movement. Certainly it did less to encourage adoptions than the benefactors and the local campaigners, to say nothing of Thomas Greenwood, and in her history of the early years of the county libraries Miss Carnell says that ' The county library movement was conceived and fostered by the CUKT. The LA and the profession were conspicuous by their absence ' (E J Carnell *County libraries* (Grafton, 1938) 31). It is only fair to point out, however, that the LA had tried for some years to remove rate limitation.

Starting seventy years after the urban libraries, county libraries should have made a better beginning. But even with the help of the CUKT they had to endure a long period of struggle. Progress was hindered by the false assumptions that county libraries could be run cheaply and that they existed to provide a service for rural areas only. At least one county library began with a farthing rate. Some county librarians were quick to realise that a good service could not be based on boxes of books in the care of volunteer librarians. The introduction of differential rating yielded some benefits, but the principle was bad.

In October 1924, the Board of Education appointed a departmental committee, under the chairmanship of Sir Frederic Kenyon, to enquire into the state of the public library service and the best means of extending it in England and Wales. The *Kenyon report* (1927) was the first government report on the public library service. To library historians it is the Domesday Book of the public library movement. Its value as an historical document lies in its detailed and revealing statistics, which show that the service was uneven and under-developed. Doubtless the economic state of the country did not encourage bold recommendations and the *Kenyon report* is more a milestone than a turning point. One well-known public librarian was bitterly disappointed and said so. To J P Lamb it was a ' singularly innocuous report '. ' The Committee ', he said, ' have a pathetic and quite unwarranted faith in local authorities ' ('A disappointing report' *Library assistant* XX August 1927 173-177). The point of this observation is that the Kenyon committee offered hopeful advice to local authorities, instead of firm recommendations to the government. It has been suggested that the *Kenyon report* did lead to some improvement in public libraries, but it is clear from the British sections of Lionel R McColvin (*ed*) *A survey of libraries* (LA, 1938) and the *McColvin report* (1942) that the improvement was very small.

During the inter-war years, however, a few libraries did progress. One notable achievement was the inauguration of special services to industry and commerce by several of the large city libraries of the midlands and the north (see J P Lamb *Commercial and technical libraries* (Allen & Unwin, 1955, chapter I).

During the 1930's, England and Wales was covered by a national-regional system of library co-operation. This was a source of general satisfaction at the time (see L Stanley Jast *The library and the community* (Nelson, 1939) chapter X), but its limitations were exposed in the 1940's by Lionel McColvin and the *Vollans report* (1952).

Several librarians who had joined the public library service during the latter years of the penny rate period were fortunate enough to be able to develop their libraries after the first world war, among them Stanley Jast (1868-1944), city librarian of Manchester and J P Lamb (1891-1969), city librarian of Sheffield. On Jast see W G Fry and W A Munford *Louis Stanley Jast* (LA, 1966) and on Lamb the biographical study by Elizabeth Melrose in W L Saunders (*ed*) *The provision and uses of library and documentation services* (Pergamon Press, 1966).

During the second world war, the public library service was given new responsibilities and did not shirk them. Even the impoverished county libraries did excellent work, mostly through sheer improvisation.

The LA's war-time Emergency Committee shared the popular conviction that the post-war world must be a better world. So many of the ideas in the *McColvin report* have become part of our current thinking that it is hard to realise that the report was viewed with some alarm by the LA, which hesitated, at first, to publish it itself, and that its own document, *The public library service: its post-war reorganization and development* (LA, 1943), which was based on the *McColvin report*, had a hostile reception at the 1946 LA conference (see Philip M Whiteman

'The McColvin Report—25 years after' *The library world*
LXIX (808) October 1967 91-96).

The first post-war governments were too busy to pay attention
to the problems of the public library service, but the *McColvin
report* and the LA's proposals did eventually become stepping
stones to the *Roberts report* (1959), the *Bourdillon report* (1962)
and the *Public Libraries and Museums Act* 1964.

The 1960's were eventful in many ways. Apart from the Act,
and the subsequent establishment of permanent advisory councils by the government, in the intervals between financial crises
much more money was available to the public library service
than ever before. One effect of this was an unprecedented expansion of the county library service. In the early days of the county
service, almost any borough librarian regarded himself and his
library as more fortunate than the neighbouring county library.
In several areas of the country the situation has now been re-
versed. K A Stockham has said ' The years 1960 to 1969 saw the
greatest volume of capital expenditure in public library history,
counties having by far the larger share '.

The recent jubilee of the county library service has been
marked by the publication of useful outline histories of it. See
K A Stockham *(ed) British county libraries 1919-1969* (Deutsch,
1969) chapters 1 and 2 and the bibliography in chapter 5, and
the symposia on county libraries in *The library world* LXX
(827) May 1969 and the *Library Association record* 71 (12) December 1969, especially the paper by Miss L V Paulin in the latter.

History embraces what happened yesterday, as well as what
happened years ago. But the recent history of public libraries
lies outside the scope of this book, as it is covered elsewhere in
this series, by George Jefferson's *Public library administration*
(Bingley, second edition 1969).

Although public libraries have existed for a much shorter
period of time than cathedral libraries, parochial libraries, subscription libraries and circulating libraries, because they are
numerous, and because they have not withered away, the literature about them already published is considerable and the facts
which remain to be brought to light incalculable.

Several substantial theses have been written on the history of individual public libraries, but the published histories are mostly very slight.

References have been made above to the work of the CUKT and to library co-operation. Neither of these relates solely to the history of public libraries, but it is convenient to mention here the principal sources of information on them. On the CUKT's library activities see William Robertson *Welfare in trust* (CUKT, 1964) and the CUKT's annual reports. The history of library co-operation, although relatively short, is extremely complicated. Fortunately there is now a lucid and comprehensive account of it in G Jefferson *Library co-operation* (Deutsch, second edition 1968), which includes a substantial classified bibliography.

George Jefferson has said 'A precise definition of public library purpose is being sought in much the same spirit as the ancient search for the philosopher's stone, and it is proving to be as elusive, as inconclusive, and perhaps as meaningless ' (*Public library administration* 7). The truth is that every generation must, and will, look for some purpose in what it is doing. Those who have the patience to discover Edward Edwards' views on public library purpose will find them surprisingly modern. For one thing, he said that public libraries must be class-less, which they did not become until this present century. Edwards would have been pleased with the 1964 Act, and I fancy he would have been delighted to know that, in the year 1970, public librarians were considering how best they might lend their support to an Open University.

No reference has been made in the above outline of public library history to Scotland, which has had its own library legislation. See W R Aitken *History of the public library movement in Scotland* (1955).

The public library history of Ireland has been outlined in Maura Neylon and Monica Henchy *Public libraries in Ireland* (University College Dublin School of Librarianship, 1966), which includes a table of statutes and a bibliography.

CHAPTER TEN

NATIONAL PUBLIC LIBRARIES

The national libraries of the world came into existence in various ways and over a long period of time. Several of them did not begin as public libraries, but became so by decree.

Irwin points out (*The heritage of the English library* chapter XII) that the need for a national library in England was realised long before the British Museum Library was established. As we have seen, the opportunity to start a national library with books from the monasteries was lost. Fortunately, the Bodleian Library, which was opened in 1602, was not restricted to the use of Oxford scholars. It was soon referred to as a public library and ' its reputation as our one national library survived till the founding of the British Museum ' (Irwin). In 1610 the Lambeth Palace Library was founded. This was also accessible to the public, but the need for a truly national public library was not met until the eighteenth century.

The British Museum was founded by Act of Parliament in 1753 and its library was opened in 1759. The library was based on four valuable collections which had hitherto been private collections. Two had been acquired by purchase (the Sloane and Harleian collections) and two by gift (the Cottonian collection and the Old Royal Library, which was given to the museum by George II). The priceless collection of Sir Robert Cotton had been the nation's property since 1700, but until the BM was founded it was inadequately housed and cared for.

The BM Library made little progress during its first sixty years. The staff were dedicated to ' peaceful and pensionless public service ' and the stock grew very slowly, as it was not until 1814 that the BM was formally given the privilege of legal deposit.

The gift of George III's library (the King's Library), in 1823, was not only important in itself, but it led to immediate action to provide the museum with a larger and safer building. The work continued for some years, but was well under way when Panizzi joined the staff, in 1831, as an assistant keeper.

Sir Anthony Panizzi (1797-1879) had been called by Arundell Esdaile 'the most creative mind in the history of the British Museum Library'. The work by which he is best remembered was done as Keeper of Printed Books, 1837-1856. Panizzi rigidly enforced legal deposit, obtained an annual grant for book purchases, planned a new reading room and iron stack and secured pensions and better salaries for the staff. In 1856 he was deservedly appointed Principal Librarian, but in 1866 he was obliged to resign through ill-health.

Panizzi's achievements are the more extraordinary in that he had to face continuous opposition. He did not lack friends, but he always had to contend with enemies, some of them (Sir Frederic Madden, in particular) on the staff of the museum.

There were two searching parliamentary enquiries into the BM Library during Panizzi's period of service. The first, the Select Committee enquiry 1835-1836, gave Panizzi (then only an assistant keeper) a welcome opportunity to state his views on the library's functions. The second, the Royal Commission enquiry 1847-1849, was an ill-founded impeachment of Panizzi, fortunately unsuccessful. The basis of it was Panizzi's justifiable refusal to print the catalogue of the library. Panizzi was able to convince the trustees that if the catalogue were printed in a hurry it would not be a good catalogue.

Panizzi was a fine scholar and a brilliant administrator. He was just and could be generous, but he was easily irritated. Edward Edwards was a supernumerary assistant at the BM Library 1839-1850. He was never on good terms with Panizzi and Panizzi had reason enough to secure his dismissal. This unfortunate episode in library history is dealt with by Edward Miller in his biography of Panizzi, and by Dr Munford in his biography of Edwards.

Panizzi bestrides his period like a colossus, and in his shadow capable but lesser men who served the BM Library during the nineteenth century are often overlooked—men such as Thomas Watts, John Winter Jones and the younger Richard Garnett. In 1875 Garnett became Superintendent of the Reading Room.

Having urged the printing of the general catalogue, he became the first chief editor. The one task which Panizzi could not undertake was successfully accomplished during the closing years of the century.

By this time, the library was once again in need of more shelf space. Relief was obtained by transferring some of the files of newspapers to a repository at Colindale, which came into use in 1905.

When the present century opened, the reputation of the BM Library was still high, but since then there has been increasing dissatisfaction. Criticism of the BM Library has been partly stimulated by the developments which have taken place in foreign national libraries in recent years, in particular the Library of Congress.

The BM Library has been criticised for hoarding ' useless literature ', for slow service to readers, for its restricted opening hours, for not being organised into subject departments and for holding itself aloof from other libraries. Not all of these criticisms are fair, and even where they are it is not easy to apportion the blame. In their post-war reports and in their evidence to the National Libraries Committee, the trustees have made it clear that they blame the government for not giving the museum an adequate income. Thus: ' The two themes of shortage of space and shortage of funds run like a dreary counterpoint through the whole story of the British Museum's attempts to give readers the service they need ' (*Principal documentary evidence submitted to the National Libraries Committee* vol 1 17).

Unexpectedly, the *Parry report* on university libraries (1967) included recommendations on the future development of the BM Library. In summary, the report said that the BM Library should be the apex of the library system of the country, which few librarians would deny.

The National Libraries Committee (commonly known as the ' Dainton committee ', after its chairman, Dr F S Dainton) was appointed in 1967 to resolve the dispute between the government and the museum's trustees over the best site for a new building for the national library. The publication of the *Report of the National Libraries Committee* (HMSO, 1969) and the *Principal documentary evidence submitted to the National Libraries Committee* (HMSO, two volumes 1969) has provoked one of the fiercest controversies in the BM's history.

The best introductions to the history of the BM Library are Arundell Esdaile and F J Hill *National libraries of the world* (LA, second edition 1957) 1-27 and F J Hill ' The British Museum Library' *The library world* LXII (726) December 1960 129-135. The standard history is Arundell Esdaile *The British Museum Library* (Allen & Unwin, 1946), an invaluable work which covers not only the history of the library but also the history of its foundation and other notable collections. Arundell Esdaile (1880-1956) was Secretary of the Museum 1926-1940. There are two other useful but less comprehensive histories: G F Barwick *The reading room of the British Museum* (Benn, 1929), and G B Rawlings *The British Museum Library* (Grafton, 1916).

The early history of the BM Library is outlined in Thomas Kelly *Early public libraries* chapter VII. The history of the foundation collections and of the library itself up to the 1860's is covered in detail by Edward Edwards *Lives of the founders of the British Museum* (1870; reprinted Amsterdam, Gerard Th Van Heusden, 1969).

Panizzi is in the DNB, but the best introduction to his work at the BM is the excellent paper by the late C B Oldman ' Sir Anthony Panizzi and the British Museum Library' *English libraries 1800-1850* (H K Lewis, 1958) 5-32. For many years, the standard biography of Panizzi was Louis Fagan *The life of Sir Anthony Panizzi* (Remington, two volumes 1880), but this has now been superseded by Edward Miller *Prince of librarians* (Andre Deutsch, 1967), which makes good use of archive material hitherto unexplored. Angus Wilson described Miller's book as a muted biography, but it tells a complicated story with skill and authority.

On the recent history of the BM Library (not covered by Esdaile) see British Museum *Report of the trustees* 1966 (1967), which covers the previous twenty five years, and British Museum *Report of the trustees 1966-1969* (1970).

For nearly 250 years, what is now the National Library of Scotland was the Advocates' Library, the library of the Scottish bar. In 1680, the Faculty of Advocates decided to devote part of its funds to buying ' the finest lawyers' and other rare books '. The library's eighteenth century history is particularly interesting. It not only acquired the deposit privilege (1709), but it came under the direction of two distinguished scholar librarians, namely, Thomas Ruddiman (1674-1757, librarian 1730-1752) and David Hume the philosopher (1711-1776, librarian 1752-1757).

By making the library freely accessible to non-members the faculty provided Scotland with a library which was national in spirit and in function long before it became national by name and law.

Legal deposit, which helped it to become one of the greatest research libraries in Europe, brought inevitable difficulties in its train. By the middle of the nineteenth century, when deposit first became really effective, the library had become a heavy burden on the resources of the faculty. Attempts were then made to obtain financial support, but without success.

In 1922, the library was offered to the nation. The government at first refused to accept it, but was later induced to do so when Sir Alexander Grant gave enough money to make it a gift without encumbrances. In 1925, the Advocates' Library became the National Library of Scotland, by Act of Parliament.

With further help from Grant, a new building was provided, but it was delayed by the war and was not completed until 1955.

It is strange that a library so old and so esteemed should have been written about so little. There is no full scale history, but the story may be pieced together from the following references: Arundell Esdaile and F J Hill *National libraries of the world* 28-38, Thomas Kelly *Early public libraries* 179-183, ' The National Library of Scotland ' *Times literary supplement* August 28 1953 555, and W K Dickson ' The Advocates' Library ' *Library Association record* new series V September 1927 169-179. On Ruddiman and Hume see Douglas Duncan *Thomas Ruddiman* (Oliver & Boyd, 1965) and M H Harris ' David Hume: scholar and librarian ' *Library quarterly* 36 (2) April 1966 88-98.

The history of the National Library of Wales is a heartening success story, notable for the generous support which the library has received from the Welsh people and the unusual qualities and qualifications of its first librarian.

The idea of a Welsh national library goes back to the eighteenth century, but it was a resolution of the National Eisteddfod of 1873 which eventually brought it into being. A committee was formed which collected books at the University College of Wales, Aberystwyth. In 1907 the library was officially brought into being by the grant of a royal charter, which gave the library the specific responsibility of collecting Welsh and Celtic material. But the deposit privilege, which was conferred in 1911, did not by any means restrict the library's claim to material of this kind, as some writers have said.

The choice of John Ballinger (1860-1933) as the first librarian was entirely against the tradition of such appointments, as he was not a graduate and his professional career had been spent entirely in public libraries. From 1880-1884 he was librarian of Doncaster and from 1884-1908 librarian of Cardiff, where he transformed a backward public library system into one of the best in the country. Ballinger's work at Cardiff explains his appointment as librarian of the National Library of Wales and he was soon to show that he had ideal qualifications for the post.

Ballinger took office in 1909. When he retired, in 1930, he left behind him a flourishing library. He raised funds for the permanent building, helped to secure the deposit privilege, gave the library an active role in library co-operation and made it a centre for summer schools in librarianship. For some years he was an active councillor of the Library Association. He never lost interest in the local public library service and was a member of the Board of Education's Committee on Public Libraries (the Kenyon committee). His knighthood was well deserved. Ballinger retired from the National Library of Wales late in life and died without having recorded his memories of the library's early years.

The National Library of Wales has been fortunate in its benefactors. Among its foundation collections was the magnificent

Welsh library of Sir John Williams, which he built up with the express intention of making it a national collection.

Although the National Library of Wales is not a state-owned library, it receives an essential annual grant from the Treasury. It is fortunate, among national libraries, in having ample room for extension, but like our other national libraries its income is inadequate.

There are several outline histories of the National Library of Wales, but no detailed history, except for the early years. See Arundell Esdaile and F J Hill *National libraries of the world* 38-48, E D Jones ' The National Library of Wales' *The library world* 62 (728) February 1961 177-181 and 'The National Library of Wales' *Times literary supplement* July 10 1953 452. The early years are chronicled in Sir W Ll Davies *The National Library of Wales* (National Library of Wales, 1937).

There is no biography of Ballinger and he is not in the DNB. See the obituary notices in the *Library Association record* third series III February 1933 43-48.

OTHER BRITISH NATIONAL LIBRARIES

The government has often been criticised for not giving greater financial support to the British Museum Library. The criticisms are just, but it should not be forgotten that for some years the government has provided, or aided by regular grants, several other libraries for direct or indirect use by the public. Apart from the National Library of Scotland, which it owns, and the National Library of Wales, which it aids, the government supports the following public libraries.

The library of the Victoria and Albert Museum has been available to the public since 1852, before it was housed at the v and A. The library of the Patent Office was opened to the public in 1855. In 1966 it was taken over by the British Museum and is now the National Reference Library of Science and Invention (Holborn Division). (The NRLSI at present exists in two physically separate units. The other part of it is called the NRLSI (Bayswater Division).) The Science Library, at the Science Museum, was built up by degrees during the nineteenth century. It had its origins in the 1840's and by the end of the century was being used as a public reference library. During the inter-war years, under the direction of the late Dr S C Bradford, the Science Library began to assume the role of a national lending library. By the 1940's the demands made upon it for loans and photo-copies were more than it could bear. It was then decided to relieve the Science Library of these responsibilities by creating a new organisation, called the National Lending Library for Science and Technology. The NLL began in 1956 as the Lending Library Unit of the former Department of Scientific and Industrial Research. The NLL became fully operational in 1962 at its present site in Yorkshire (Boston Spa).

The National Central Library was founded in 1916 as the Central Library for Students. In 1930, having been given wider responsibilities, it was re-named the National Central Library. NCL is a chartered institution, but since 1930 it has been grant aided by the Treasury. The functions of NCL (according to its charter) are to act as a national lending library and as a central clearing house for loans of books between all types of libraries.

Information on the history of these other national libraries will be found in Raymond Irwin and Ronald Staveley (eds) *The libraries of London* (LA, second edition 1961), J Burkett (ed) *Special library and information services in the United Kingdom* (LA, second edition, 1965), L M Harrod *The libraries of greater London* (Bell, 1951), George Jefferson *Library co-operation* (Deutsch, second edition 1968), and M W Hill ' The National Reference Library of Science and Invention' *The library world* LXXI (832) October 1969 99-105.

NATIONAL LIBRARY OF IRELAND

Probably because it is a late foundation and, unlike the library of Trinity College, Dublin, does not receive British books under the law of legal deposit, the National Library of Ireland is not as well known to British librarians as it should be. It was originally the library of the Royal Dublin Society, which was founded in 1731. The library, which was established in the early days of the society, was purchased by the government in 1877 and thereupon became the National Library of Ireland. It is now the principal centre for research in Irish history and Irish literature. Among its librarians, one may single out the much loved and respected Thomas William Lyster (1855-1922, librarian 1895-1920). Lyster was an active member of the Library Association and the virtual founder of the LA's *Subject index to periodicals*.

See Arundell Esdaile and F J Hill *National libraries of the world* 128-133, Eric Hicks 'The National Library of Ireland' *The library world* July 1969 7-10, and Ernest A Savage 'The friendliest library in the world' *Library review* XIII (102) Summer 1952 360-367. There is a brief biography of Lyster in John Minto *A history of the public library movement in Great Britain and Ireland* (LA, 1932) 324-326.

FUNCTIONS OF NATIONAL LIBRARIES

Panizzi's views on the functions of the British Museum Library, as expressed in his evidence to the Select Committee, are well known (*English libraries 1800-1850* 14). Panizzi did not suggest that the BM Library should be the apex, or keystone, of a national library system. In Panizzi's day there was no national library system.

It was not until the present century and, indeed, until after the second world war that there was much discussion of the functions of national libraries. The first edition (1934) of *National libraries of the world* was written entirely by Arundell Esdaile. Esdaile did not include any general observations on the functions of national libraries, but in later years he recorded his views in 'The great libraries of the world and their functions' *Library review* XII (94) Summer 1950 344-349. For other references see Donald Davinson *Academic and legal deposit libraries* (Bingley, second edition 1969) chapter one.

CHAPTER ELEVEN

UNIVERSITY LIBRARIES

The history of British universities has many interesting and several curious features, an observation which also applies to the history of their libraries.

University library history falls naturally into two parts. The first concerns the libraries of the older universities, and the second the libraries of the modern foundations of the nineteenth and twentieth centuries.

The university library of Oxford began in the fourteenth century as a collection of books in a room adjoining St Mary's Church. The liberal benefactions of Humfrey, Duke of Gloucester, in the fifteenth century, called for more suitable accommodation and a handsome room, which has always been known as Duke Humfrey's Library, was built over the Divinity School. After the destruction of the books by Edward VI's commissioners, the library furniture was sold, so that when Sir Thomas Bodley (1545-1613) returned to Oxford, in the 1590's, he saw only ' a bare and desolate roome '. In 1598, Bodley offered to restore the library. His proposals were gladly accepted.

Although he had a capable librarian, Dr Thomas James (1573-1629), who has been called the greatest of all Bodley's librarians, Bodley supervised the organisation of the new library himself, with unflagging zeal, down to the last detail. The new library was opened in 1602. Bodley died in 1613, but even by then the library had made considerable progress. The first catalogue had been published, the deposit agreement had been made with the Stationers' Company and the first extension to the library building had been built.

Bodley was a model benefactor. He understood very well what needed to be done, he left the library with a good income and his generosity and single-minded devotion to his library inspired devotion and generosity in others.

By the eve of the Civil War, which brought the library no harm, further extensions had been completed and the Bodleian had become one of the finest libraries in Europe.

The eighteenth century was a period of weak administration and little growth, but between the Napoleonic wars and the first world war the stock increased sixfold. This century was spanned by three remarkable librarians, Bulkeley Bandinel (librarian 1813-1860), Henry Octavious Coxe (librarian 1860-1882) and Edward W B Nicholson (1848-1912, librarian 1882-1912).

Nicholson's term of office was stormy but productive. Unwilling to delegate responsibility and always at loggerheads with the curators, he nevertheless achieved a drastic and much needed re-organisation of the library. He will always be remembered, at Oxford, as an uncompromising and rather eccentric personality and, by the library profession, as the founder of the Library Association.

In the latter part of the nineteenth century, when the publishers could no longer evade the obligations of legal deposit, the stock of the Bodleian Library grew rapidly. The need for more accommodation was only temporarily alleviated by the acquisition of the Radcliffe Camera and the provision of an underground book store. Eventually, with the help of the Rockefeller Foundation, a large extension (New Library) was built in the 1930's and opened in 1946.

' Of all the great libraries of this country ', said Dr Myres, ' the Bodleian bears the marks of its history most deeply upon it '. This is true, but even so it is surprising to find that the history of the library has been written so often. (See E H Cordeaux and D H Merry *A bibliography of the printed works relating to the University of Oxford* (OUP, 1968) 466-469.)

Pride of place must be given to two remarkable but dissimilar works: W D Macray *Annals of the Bodleian Library Oxford* (OUP, second edition 1890), a detailed chronology from foundation to 1880, and Sir Edmund Craster *History of the Bodleian Library 1845-1945* (OUP, 1952), which Arundell Esdaile called ' the most readable and rewarding book that has yet been written on library history '. (Sir Edmund was Bodley's librarian 1931-1945.) Detailed

University Library ' *Times literary supplement* March 26 1954 207.

On Henry Bradshaw see G W Prothero *Henry Bradshaw* (Kegan Paul, 1888), John L Thornton *Selected readings in the history of librarianship* chapter 18 and the DNB. On Francis Jenkinson see H F Stewart *Francis Jenkinson* (CUP, 1926) and the DNB. The DNB article on Jenkinson, by Sir Stephen Gaselee, includes the striking observation ' Few librarians excel both as scholars and administrators '. Exceptions may surely be found in the history of the university libraries of Oxford and Cambridge.

OXFORD AND CAMBRIDGE COLLEGE LIBRARIES

The college libraries of Oxford and Cambridge are of singular interest and importance. Nearly all of the older colleges have substantial collections built up from the fifteenth century. They have profited greatly from gifts and are rich in manuscripts and early printed books. N R Ker *Medieval libraries of Great Britain* (Royal Historical Society, second edition 1964) shows that several of these libraries have a fair number of books from the monasteries. The most notable example is Corpus Christi College, Cambridge, which has Archbishop Parker's collection. Cambridge has also become the permanent home of the famous private library of Samuel Pepys, which was presented to Magdalene College in 1724.

The general sources of information on the college libraries of Oxford and Cambridge include Landau's *Encyclopaedia* (see under ' University College libraries '), J W Clark *The care of books*, B H Streeter *The chained library* and Francis Wormald and C E Wright *The English library before 1700* chapters X and XI.

On the college libraries of Oxford, see also Strickland Gibson *Some Oxford libraries* and N R Ker ' Oxford college libraries in the sixteenth century ' *Bodleian Library record* 6 (3) January 1959 459-515, and on the college libraries of Cambridge A N L Munby *Cambridge college libraries* (Heffer, second edition 1962).

In the 1960's, there was much discussion on the functions and future development of the university libraries of Oxford and

Cambridge. At both universities special investigating committees were appointed and each committee has published a substantial report—University of Oxford *Report of the Committee on University Libraries* (1966), commonly known as the *Shackleton report,* and 'First report of the General Board's Committee on Libraries' *Cambridge University reporter* XCIX (29) March 28 1969.

LIBRARY OF TRINITY COLLEGE DUBLIN
The library of Trinity College, Dublin, is one of the greatest libraries in the western world. It is rich in treasures, which include the *Book of Kells.* When the University of Dublin was founded, in 1591, it was intended that it should consist of several colleges, but Trinity was the only one established. The library is almost exactly contemporary with the Bodleian. Esdaile's intriguing remark, in his introduction to Burton's *Famous libraries of the world,* that this is the only library to have been founded by an army, seems to have no basis in fact. Archbishop James Ussher took a great interest in the library and it eventually acquired his own private collection, in a roundabout way. During the eighteenth century, when the university libraries of Oxford and Cambridge made little progress, the library of Trinity College prospered. One of the librarians during this century was George Berkeley, the philosopher. The deposit privilege, conferred in 1801, inevitably created a need for more space and recently the library building has been extended following a successful appeal for financial aid.

See H W Parke *The library of Trinity College Dublin* (Trinity College, 1961), Margaret Burton *Famous libraries of the world* (Grafton, 1937) 60-71 and 'The library of Trinity College Dublin' *Times literary supplement* March 16 1956 172.

MODERN UNIVERSITY LIBRARIES
By the end of the sixteenth century, Scotland had four universities and England had two. There were no other foundations for nearly 250 years. Durham University was chartered in 1832 and London University in 1836. The next one hundred years saw the

struggling beginnings of twelve 'civic universities'. All of them began as impoverished university colleges and most of them had to wait for some years before they became autonomous. The universities which have been founded since the second world war have fortunately escaped the chrysalis university college stage.

When the University Grants Committee was established in 1919, conditions in the libraries of the modern universities were most unsatisfactory and the early reports of the UGC had much to complain of. For example: ' With a few exceptions the libraries of our universities and colleges are suffering a process of starvation, and large additional sums will have to be spent upon them before they could be regarded as maintained on a scale commensurate with their real needs' (UGC *Returns* 1921-22 6).

When this was written, the stocks of these libraries were inadequate, the staffs small and underpaid and the library accommodation was in most instances unsuitable. Several libraries had no full time university librarian and where there was one it seldom happened that he had been accorded professorial status. By the 1930's, there had been some improvement, due partly to the help and encouragement of the UGC, and partly to the individual and co-operative efforts of the librarians themselves. The Joint Standing Committee on Library Co-operation was set up in 1925 and the University and Research Section of the Library Association was formed in 1927. But in the years between the two world wars, ' large additional sums ' could not be found to spend on our universities and the progress made by university libraries in the 1930's seems very small in comparison with the developments of the 1960's.

Post war development, slow at first, has greatly accelerated since the late 1950's and the libraries of the recently founded universities have had a much better start than those of the older ' redbrick ' universities.

Little work has been done on the library history of the modern universities, and it is difficult, at present, to trace even the outline. See Landau's *Encyclopaedia of librarianship* (' University libraries '), B S Page ' University library development ' *Proceedings of the annual conference of the Library Association 1957* 52-58 and

E G Baxter 'A preliminary historical survey of developments in university libraries in Great Britain 1919-1950' *Library Association record* 56 (9 and 10) September and October 1954 330-335 and 389-393, and the quinquennial reports of the UGC.

Some idea of the difficulties with which the libraries of the modern universities have had to contend may be gained from J A Rigg 'A comparative history of the libraries of Manchester and Liverpool Universities up to 1903' in W L Saunders (*ed*) *University and research library studies* (Pergamon Press, 1968) and the sections on the library of Leicester University (formerly Leicester University College) in Jack Simmons *New university* (Leicester University Press, 1958).

In the 1960's there was considerable discussion on the functions and desirable developments of university libraries. Much of this discussion was stimulated by the publication of University Grants Committee *Report of the Committee on Libraries* (HMSO, 1967), commonly referred to as the *Parry report,* after the name of the chairman of the committee, Dr Thomas Parry. For references to this report and other recent publications on the functions of university libraries see Donald Davinson *Academic and legal deposit libraries* (Bingley, second edition 1969).

CHAPTER TWELVE

LEGAL DEPOSIT

In the two previous chapters, several references have been made to the law of legal deposit. As the deposit privilege has been frequently attacked for many years, its history is worth considering at greater length.

The idea of legal deposit was conceived in France. It began in 1537 with the Montpellier Ordinance of Francis I, which was intended to enrich the royal library. Since then, similar measures have been passed in most countries of the world.

In England, legal deposit was preceded by voluntary deposit. The arrangement which Bodley made with the Stationers' Company in 1610 was no more than a gentleman's agreement. Why the company favoured it is not clear, but its members soon regretted the arrangement and were at no great pains to honour it.

In 1637 deposit at the Bodleian Library became obligatory by a Star Chamber decree, but when the Star Chamber was abolished, in 1640, deposit once again became voluntary. Legal deposit returned with the Press Licensing Act of 1662, which gave the privilege to the Royal Library and Cambridge University Library, as well as to the Bodleian Library. The main intention of this Act was not to help these libraries, but to bring to the notice of the authorities blasphemous and seditious literature. This Act was renewed at intervals, but when it lapsed in 1695 the House of Commons refused to renew it for a further period.

A few years later, the publishers pleaded for copyright protection and obtained it in the Copyright Act 1709, but at the expense of nine deposited copies. These were for the benefit of the three original deposit libraries, together with the library of Sion College, London, the libraries of the four Scottish universities and of the recently established library of the Faculty of Advocates, Edinburgh (the Act of Union with Scotland had been passed in 1707).

The publishers, who had contrived to avoid deposit under the Press Licensing Acts, continued to avoid it under the Copyright

Act. Nevertheless, by the Act of 1801 two Irish libraries, the libraries of Trinity College and King's Inn, Dublin, were added to the deposit list ' to commemorate the union with Ireland '.

Although the Copyright Act 1814 did not change the number of deposit libraries, it belatedly established the right of the British Museum to deposit. (The Trustees of the BM had always been in doubt as to whether the deposit privilege had been transferred to the museum with the gift of the old Royal Library in 1757, and as late as 1806 had found it necessary to consult the Master of the Rolls on this matter.)

The 1814 Act inaugurated a long period of agitation by the publishers for relief from what they had always regarded as a unique and unfair tax. In 1836 they achieved a partial success. By the Copyright Act of that year, the number of deposit libraries was reduced to five—the British Museum Library, the Bodleian Library, Cambridge University Library, the library of the Faculty of Advocates and the library of Trinity College, Dublin. The six libraries which lost the privilege were awarded a small annual grant by the government as compensation.

Evasion still continued, but not for long. In the 1850's, Panizzi obtained powers from the BM trustees to serve writs on defaulting publishers. Within ten years the annual intake of deposited books at the museum doubled. Panizzi did not stop short at hounding the London publishers. He turned his attention also to those in the provinces.

In 1859, inspired by Panizzi's example, the other copyright libraries took action. In 1863 they jointly appointed an efficient agent to claim books on their behalf. Since then, there has been no large-scale evasion of deposit.

By the Copyright Act 1911, a sixth library was added to the list, the new National Library of Wales. Since 1911, there has been no major change in the deposit law. The National Library of Scotland inherited the privilege from the Faculty of Advocates, and by mutual agreement between the governments of the UK and Ireland the library of Trinity College retains the privilege, in return for the deposit of Irish books at the five British copyright libraries.

In 1951, the President of the Board of Trade appointed a committee to consider whether any changes were desirable in the copyright law. In doing so, the committee took note of section 15 of the Copyright Act 1911, which dealt with legal deposit. After hearing evidence from the copyright libraries and the Publishers' Association, the committee decided to recommend that no change should be made in the deposit law ' in view of the long-standing nature of the privilege and obligation, and what we feel to be the comparatively small burden it creates for the publishing trade as a whole in relation to their turnover '. The government accepted this advice and the deposit section of the Copyright Act 1911 remains unrepealed.

The *Report of the copyright committee* was published in 1952. Since then, the deposit law has been several times attacked by authors and publishers. In 1962 I wrote ' Our publishers might be a little reconciled towards legal deposit if they were occasionally reminded by the copyright libraries of the considerable extent to which these libraries have benefited and still benefit, from the deposit privilege '. But if the publishers were to visit the stacks of the copyright libraries it is most unlikely that they would be reconciled. By law, the British Museum must have a copy of every publication. The other copyright libraries receive only what they request, but for some years they have requested almost every book and restrict their requests only for newspapers and periodicals. Many of the books have so far had little or no use. But it is difficult to foresee the demands of scholars of the future, and none of the copyright libraries would readily surrender the deposit privilege unless it had ample financial compensation from the government in lieu.

Although it has long been the custom to refer to the deposit libraries as ' copyright libraries ', as the Copyright Committee pointed out ' it is not a question of copyright so-called '. As long ago as 1798, it was ruled in the Court of King's Bench that copyright in a publication was not forfeited if the publisher failed to deliver copies for deposit. It might be expected that making copyright dependent on deposit would be the best way of securing the deposit of every publication, but the experience of countries where such a law exists does not confirm this theory.

Although the history of legal deposit is dull in outline, it is interesting in detail. The proof of this will be found in R C Barrington Partridge *The history of the legal deposit of books throughout the British Empire* (LA, 1938), a unique work of impeccable scholarship. Part I deals with deposit in Great Britain and Ireland. Partridge has also written on the subject briefly in Landau's *Encyclopaedia of librarianship* and in ' The history of the copyright privilege in England ' *Library Association record* third series II February and March 1932 41-48 73-83.

An account of Panizzi's enforcement of legal deposit will be found in Partridge chapter VII, and in Edward Miller *Prince of librarians* (Deutsch, 1967) chapter 11. On the joint action of the other copyright libraries see Sir Edmund Craster *History of the Bodleian Library 1845-1945* (OUP, 1952) 61-64.

The arguments which have been advanced for and against legal deposit over the centuries are summarised and reviewed in J G Ollé ' Free books in an affluent society ' *The library world* LXIV (750) December 1962 162-167. See also Board of Trade *Report of the Copyright Committee* (HMSO, 1952) part IV, and C H Rolph ' Lost deposits?' *Times literary supplement* 3393 March 9 1967 183-184.

CHAPTER THIRTEEN

SPECIAL LIBRARIES

It is difficult to survey the general history of special libraries. This is partly because there are so many different kinds of special libraries, but the major difficulty is that there is still a great deal of work to be done in this area of library history.

It is probable that more has been written on the history of individual special libraries than we are aware of, for it often happens that when individual histories are published they appear in books and periodicals outside the literature of librarianship.

Furthermore, there is no generally accepted definition of 'special library'. Kelly does not use the term. In his classification of libraries (*Early public libraries* appendix I), special libraries are covered by the wider term 'institutional libraries'. In this chapter I have used the term 'special libraries' to include the libraries of learned societies, professional associations, government departments and the libraries of nationalised industries, industrial research associations and private firms.

A scrutiny of John L Thornton *The chronology of librarianship* and the historical notes in L M Harrod *The libraries of Greater London* (Bell, 1951) shows that several well-known libraries which are commonly regarded as 'special' have a long history. Our oldest special libraries came into existence in the sixteenth century. The exact dates of foundation are not always known, but during this century were established the libraries of the Royal College of Physicians, Gray's Inn and the Inner Temple.

In the year 1586, or thereabouts, the first Society of Antiquaries was established. The society hoped to found an academy of antiquarian and historical studies 'well furnished with ancient books', but the society faded away and this proposal came to nothing (see Irwin's *The heritage of the English library* 226).

The first successful learned society was the Royal Society of London. This was founded in 1660 and its library was started soon afterwards. (Actually, the Royal Society was not so much a learned society, in its early days, as a gentlemen's club for the amiable discussion of scientific matters.)

Learned societies remained few in number, however, until the latter half of the eighteenth century, when a movement began to establish national and local scientific societies and local literary and philosophical societies, which often had strong scientific interests (see Thomas Kelly *A history of adult education in Great Britain* chapter 7). These societies often had a library and a museum.

By the middle of the nineteenth century, professional associations began to multiply and these also established libraries, for example the libraries of the Law Society (1828), the Royal Institute of British Architects (1834) and the Institution of Mechanical Engineers (1847).

The early history of government libraries is still obscure, but a few of them had their origins in the nineteenth century. Owing to the merging of ministries in recent years, and the consequent merging of their libraries, the history of government departmental libraries is not straightforward.

By the beginning of the present century, the need for many more special libraries was becoming recognised, and in discussions on this subject the term ' special libraries ' was first brought into general use.

The first world war brought home to the government the undeniable fact that this country was lagging behind in scientific and industrial research. To remedy this situation, in 1916 the government founded the Department of Scientific and Industrial Research. This brought into being a number of government research stations and grant-aided industrial research associations, each with its library.

Before the first world war, there were hardly any libraries in this country owned by private firms. Only a small number came into existence in the inter-war years. The establishment of the Association of Special Libraries and Information Bureaux (later officially re-named Aslib) in 1924 was very much an act of faith. In its early years, while it was trying to interest commerce and industry in library and information services, it had great difficulty in securing its own existence.

The lessons which had not been learned in the first world war were learned in the second. Since 1945 there has been a remarkable increase in the number of scientific and industrial libraries. There has also been a considerable increase in the number of government departmental libraries (see J Burkett (ed) *Special library and information services in the United Kingdom* chapter 2).

The unprecedented growth of special libraries since the second world war has affected the library profession in two ways. It has drawn away from the public library service many experienced librarians, and it has helped to change the composition of the membership of the Library Association. For many years, the LA had been virtually an association of public librarians. It is no longer so.

The only attempt which has been made to write a history of special libraries in Britain is Ada Winifred Johns *Special libraries* (Scarecrow Press, 1968) 13-64. This is of very limited value. The sources drawn upon have not been used to the best advantage and the author's definition of a special library is rather narrow.

The only profitable way to study the history of special libraries is to investigate each type separately. But not many types can be investigated without difficulty. The exceptions are medical and scientific libraries. On these see John L Thornton *Medical books libraries and collectors* (Deutsch, second edition 1966), and John L Thornton and R I J Tully *Scientific books libraries and collectors* (LA, second edition 1962).

When working on the history of other kinds of special libraries, some information may be gleaned from the following general sources: Thornton's *Chronology,* the various editions of the *Aslib directory* (the first was published in 1928), J Burkett (ed) *Special library and information services in the United Kingdom* (LA, second edition, 1965), Raymond Irwin and Ronald Staveley (eds) *The libraries of London* (LA, second edition 1966), L M Harrod *The libraries of Greater London* (Bell, 1951) and Reginald Arthur Rye *The students' guide to the libraries of London* (University of London Press, third edition 1928). On scientific and industrial libraries see also Roland Astall *Special libraries and information bureaux* (Bingley, 1966) chapter 1 and D J Foskett *Information service in libraries* (Crosby Lockwood, second edition, 1967) chapter 1.

The future of special library history is uncertain. For obvious reasons, the archives of government departments, learned societies, private firms, and so forth, cannot be made freely accessible to outsiders. Therefore, unless the librarians of special libraries choose to work on the history of the libraries under their control, the history of British libraries will remain incomplete.

CHAPTER FOURTEEN

PRIVATE LIBRARIES

Raymond Irwin points out (*The English library* 173) that there are two kinds of private libraries. One is the imposing library born of wealth and the acquisitive instinct. The other is the small and homelier collection ' gathered for the purpose of individual study or personal enjoyment '. This second type Irwin calls the ' domestic library ' and it is the domestic library whose history he has traced so engagingly in *The English library*. In this chapter we are concerned with the first type.

Unless they are themselves bibliophiles, librarians are likely to be little interested in the great private collections of the past, except where they have survived to enrich our public and institutional libraries. But many famous private libraries have been dispersed, and the few that still remain in private hands have been whittled away by taxation, like the library of the dukes of Devonshire at Chatsworth.

During the Middle Ages, most books belonged to institutional libraries. There were few private collections of any size in Britain before the Renaissance. A well-known exception is the library of Richard de Bury (1287-1345), Bishop of Durham, the supposed author of *Philobiblon*. Apparently Richard intended to bequeath his books to a new college at Oxford he hoped to endow, but he died in debt and his library was dispersed.

A notable collector of the fifteenth century was Humfrey, Duke of Gloucester (1391-1447). His collection was small but valuable and is chiefly remembered because part of it was given to the University Library of Oxford. Few of his books survive today.

It has been said that the golden age of book-collecting in England was from 1560 to 1640. It was during this period that priceless mss from the dispersed collections of the monasteries were retrieved by private collectors. Matthew Parker (1504-1575) used the authority of his office to obtain many of his books, but his collection was bequeathed to Corpus Christi College, Cambridge.

Sir Robert Bruce Cotton (1571-1631) was a wealthy scholar and renowned antiquary who assembled a small but unique collection of historical and literary texts. Although he was extremely proud of his library, which he called his ' treasure house ', he allowed many scholars to make use of it and even to borrow from it. Cotton's collection was presented to the Crown (one could say it was compulsorily acquired) in 1700, and eventually became one of the foundation collections of the British Museum Library. In the intervening years it was inadequately cared for and in 1731 a part of it was destroyed by fire.

In 1627, a famous treatise on librarianship was published in France—*Advis pour dresser une bibliothèque*. The author, Gabriel Naudé (1600-1653) had a distinguished career as librarian of several private libraries, among them the great library of Cardinal Mazarin. Naudé's book was translated by John Evelyn and published in London in 1661. What influence it had on book collecting in this country it is hard to say, but his advice to wealthy collectors was that they should, among other things, employ competent librarians and make their libraries accessible to needy scholars.

The librarians of private libraries are little known. Naudé is one exception. Another is Humfrey Wanley (1672-1726), library keeper to Robert Harley (1661-1724) and Edward Harley (1689-1741), first and second earls of Oxford. The Harleys were omnivorous collectors and their extensive collection of mss was worth a good deal more than the £10,000 which the government paid for it in 1753, when it became another of the remarkable foundation collections of the British Museum Library. Wanley's diary, which has only recently been published, tells us how the collection was built up and how it was used while it was still a private library. Regrettably, the BM was unable to acquire the Harleys' printed books.

The Royal Library was started by Edward IV in the fifteenth century. It grew by fits and starts and did not develop much until the seventeenth century. In 1551, Edward VI purged it ' of all superstitutious bookes' and after the execution of Charles I proposals were made to sell it. Fortunately this did not happen. Instead, it was placed under the care of John Durie. Durie was librarian for only a few years, but in 1650, the year of his appointment, he wrote and published *The reformed librarie-keeper*, another early classic of library literature.

Under Charles II the Royal Library grew once again, but thereafter was neglected. In 1757, George II presented it to the British Museum, where it is referred to as the ' Old Royal Library ' to distinguish it from the Royal Library of George III.

The fourth of the foundation collections of the BM Library was the collection of Sir Hans Sloane (1660-1753). Sloane was a distinguished scholar and physician who instructed his executors to offer his library and his private museum to the nation for a nominal sum. The offer was accepted and the purchase of the Sloane collections was the immediate cause of the foundation of the British Museum. In comparison with the other foundation collections, the Sloane collection of books and mss had few treasures, but, as Esdaile says, the museum ' owes to him a very solid foundation-stone of a great library of universal scope '.

George II having disposed of the Royal Library, George III assembled a new one. In 1823, this substantial collection was also offered to the nation and in 1828 transferred to the BM, where the bulk of it has been kept together as the King's Library.

The nineteenth century is remarkable for the fantastically large collections of Richard Heber and Sir Thomas Phillipps. Richard Heber, ' a bibliomaniac if ever there was one ' (Seymour de Ricci), collected printed books; Sir Thomas Phillipps collected manuscripts. Phillipps was the greatest collector of manuscripts the world has ever known. Unfortunately, neither Heber nor Phillipps made arrangements for their collections to be preserved intact.

By the end of the nineteenth century, English private libraries were in decline and since then many of their treasures have been sold for the benefit of private and institutional libraries in America. One great library was saved. The library of the second Earl Spencer (1758-1834), commonly known as the Althorp Library, ranks as one of the finest libraries ever assembled by a private collector, especially for its early printed books. In 1895, it was purchased entire by Mrs George Rylands for the John Rylands Library which she was building in Manchester in memory of her husband. The John Rylands Library was opened in 1899, thus giving Manchester the distinction of having two famous endowed public libraries.

There is a large but scattered literature on private libraries. The general sources of information are W Y Fletcher *English book collectors* (Kegan Paul, 1902) and Seymour de Ricci *English collectors of books and manuscripts 1530-1930* (CUP, 1930; reprinted Holland Press, 1960).

On Richard de Bury see Raymond Irwin *The heritage of the English library* chapter X, Wormald and Wright *The English library before 1700* chapter VI and John Thornton *Selected readings in the history of librarianship* chapter 3.

On Gabriel Naudé see Raymond Irwin *The English library* chapter X, Thornton's *Selected readings* chapter 8 and J A Clarke ' Gabriel Naudé and the foundations of the scholarly library' *Library quarterly* 39 (4) October 1969 331-343. The best English translation of Naudé's book is *Advice on establishing a library* (University of California Press, 1950).

On the foundation collections of the BM Library see Thomas Kelly *Early public libraries* 152-157. On the foundation and other collections, including the King's Library, see Arundell Esdaile *The British Museum Library* (Allen & Unwin, 1946) part II and Edward Edwards *Lives of the founders of the British Museum* (1870). Esdaile's book is the most useful source of information.

Further sources of information on the individual foundation collections are as follows: Cottonian Collection, Wormald and Wright chapter IX and Hope Mirrlees *A fly in amber* (Faber, 1962) chapter III; Harleian Collection, C E Wright ' Humfrey Wanley' *Proceedings of the British Academy* 1960 99-129 and *The diary of Humfrey Wanley 1715-1726* edited by C E Wright and R C Wright (Bibliographical Society, two volumes, 1966); George II's Collection, *The Old Royal Library* (British Museum,

1957); Sloane Collection, Sir Frank Francis ' Sir Hans Sloane as a collector ' *Library Association record* 63 (1) January 1961 1-5.

The vast collection of Sir Thomas Phillipps has not been preserved entire and is still going through the long process of dispersal. The detailed studies of Phillipps and his collection by A N L Munby have been reduced into one readable volume: A N L Munby *Portrait of an obsession* (Constable, 1967).

On the John Rylands Library and the Althorp Library see Henry Guppy *The John Rylands Library Manchester 1899-1924* (Manchester University Press, 1924).

Raymond Irwin's history of the English domestic library will be found in *The English library* 173-293. See also A N L Munby *The libraries of English men of letters* (LA, 1964).

There are numerous articles on private libraries in the files of the *Library* and the *Book collector*.

CHAPTER FIFTEEN

THE LIBRARY ASSOCIATIONS

The first organised meeting of librarians anywhere took place at New York in 1853. Although it was well supported, there were no further meetings until the Philadelphia conference of 1876, when the American Library Association was founded.

In 1877, E W B Nicholson, at that time librarian of the London Institution, suggested that an international conference of librarians should be held in London. This proposal found favour and a conference was held in October 1877. On the last day, the Library Association of the United Kingdom was formed with the object of uniting ' all persons engaged or interested in library work for the purpose of promoting the best possible administration of existing libraries and the formation of new ones where desirable '. Nicholson was appointed joint secretary, with Henry Tedder, but in the following year he resigned.

In its early years the LA had a heterogeneous membership, but as it grew it recruited most of its new members from the expanding public library service. Progress was reasonably good until the end of the century, but the thirty years which followed the grant of a Royal Charter to the association, in 1898, were the worst in its history.

The story of this period is probably best known through the writings of Dr Savage, in particular from his autobiography *A librarian's memories*. In his latter years, Savage, who led the association out of the wilderness in the 1920's, could find little that was good to say about the conduct of the LA's affairs during the two previous decades. Looking for a scapegoat, he found one in Henry Tedder (1850-1924). Tedder was one of the founders of the LA and he worked for it for many years and in several capacities, in particular as Honorary Treasurer 1889-1924, except for the year when he was President. Undoubtedly Tedder was cautious and conservative, but Savage writes about him with unwarranted venom. The ills which beset the LA at the beginning of the century cannot all be ascribed to Tedder. But undeniably, the LA was in a most unsatisfactory state.

In the first place, it had failed to unite all those engaged in librarianship. This was not altogether the LA's fault, except that it had neglected to create a branch structure. A fair number of chief librarians in the provinces preferred to belong to their regional library association. There were several of these, and although they were affiliated to the LA, and the LA chose to call them ' branches', they were quite independent (see John Minto *A history of the public library movement* chapter XIV).

Few library assistants (they were not then called assistant librarians) belonged to the LA. In 1895, they founded their own association, ' to sulk and grouse in ', according to Savage. They did grouse, but they did not sulk. In fact, they handled their affairs, including the publication of their monthly journal, very well indeed. Not only was the membership fee of the LA more than most assistants could afford, but there was then a social gap between chief librarians and assistants which even Savage could not deny.

The concentration of the LA's affairs into the hands of the London councillors was due partly to lack of interest in the LA in the provinces and partly to the inability of the LA to pay the expenses of country councillors.

The LA was handicapped in many ways by its small membership. (In the ten years from 1901-1911 it rose from 593 to 655.) It could not afford a paid secretary (only an assistant secretary for clerical duties) and a considerable amount of work fell on the shoulders of the honorary officers. The association had no permanent home and moved from one address to another with disheartening frequency.

In one respect, however, the LA was fortunate. From 1905 to 1915 it had a popular and energetic Honorary Secretary, Stanley Jast. But even Jast could be pessimistic about the future of the association. In 1911, at the Perth annual conference, he suggested that the LA should amalgamate with ' kindred associations ', by which he meant the Museums Association, the Bibliographical Society and the Library Assistants' Association. In that same year, the LA had to endure the resignation from membership of one of its most distinguished members, James Duff Brown.

After the first world war, the LA's situation grew even worse. Savage's comment in the *Annals of the Library Association* for December 1922 reads as follows: 'At this time the Association was at its lowest period of prosperity, notwithstanding, and partly on account of, the increase of subscriptions in 1919. The Assistant Secretary was not replaced. The *Record* became a quarterly instead of a monthly periodical'.

Reformation began in 1926. In that year, Savage's motion for a special committee to report on the development of the association was approved. In 1928, Savage himself became Honorary Secretary. Over the next five years the LA was transformed.

In 1903, at the suggestion of James Duff Brown, the LA had asked Carnegie to provide the association with a headquarters building and enough money to support it. Carnegie curtly refused. In 1929, the CUKT agreed to provide the LA with a series of grants and on the strength of this welcome offer the LA's plans for re-organisation went through without a hitch. The independent associations (with the exception of Aslib) amalgamated with the LA. The Association of Assistant Librarians, as the LAA was then called, became a section of the LA as from January 1930. (At the time of amalgamation, it was almost as large as the LA.) Also, from January 1930, librarians were not permitted to sit for LA examinations unless they were members of the association. In 1931, the *Record* resumed monthly publication. In 1933, the LA took possession of Chaucer House, the first building it could call its own. Savage had achieved his objectives. In February 1934, he relinquished the post of Honorary Secretary. He was succeeded by Lionel Roy McColvin, who held office until 1951.

From the point at which McColvin became Honorary Secretary, the history of the LA can be traced without difficulty in the writings of Robert Vollans, Charles Nowell and D D Haslam listed below. Haslam has said that 'To more than one generation of librarians, not only in the United Kingdom but throughout the English-speaking world, the name Lionel McColvin was almost synonymous with that of the Library Association ' (*Libraries for the people* 53).

During the second world war, more ground was gained than lost, thanks to the hard working Emergency Committee and, in particular, to its industrious Honorary Secretary. The publication of the *McColvin report* in 1942 is one of the best-known events in the association's history. Since then, a much larger and more diverse membership has stimulated many changes and endorsed a new constitution.

Although the association has had a paid secretary since 1928, the office of Honorary Secretary continued until 1961, at the end of which year it was abolished. This brought to an end a long period during which the LA depended heavily, and perhaps to an unreasonable extent, on the self-sacrifice of a few of its members. A substantial biographical dictionary could be compiled of all those who have worked for the LA, not forgetting those who have edited its journals.

One of its paid officers deserves special mention. The late P S J Welsford was Secretary of the association 1931-1959, a period of expansion and change unique in the LA's history. Few members realised, at the time, how much the Secretary (or the Honorary Secretary) contributed to the association's progress.

The formation of the County Libraries Section of the LA, in 1927, inaugurated a most successful development in the association's affairs, although most of the present sections did not come into being until after the war.

As I have said, the AAL did not begin as a section of the LA, but had a vigorous life, from 1895 to 1929, as an independent association. Within a few years of its foundation, it gained the general support of public library assistants and had a national network of branches (divisions) when the LA had hardly any. At the beginning of the century, when it was called the Library Assistants' Association, it was remarkably fortunate in its officers. While Jast was struggling to keep the LA from falling to pieces, his deputy librarian, Berwick Sayers, was building up the LAA into a highly efficient association. During the period 1906-1915, Sayers was in office either as Honorary Secretary or as President of the LAA. As he said, many years later, the LAA became the central interest in his life.

Having swallowed the AAL, the LA failed to digest it and it has been able to retain its identity even after the re-organisation of the LA, which became effective in 1962. From its early days, the AAL has been especially interested in professional education and better salaries and conditions. For some years, the continued existence of this association within an association has been questioned, but so far all who have prophesied its demise have been false prophets.

In 1945 J T Gillett said ' The LA has never been able to command the respect and devotion of its members in the same way as the AAL has done in the fifty years of its existence '.

There is no full scale history of the LA, but there is a useful indexed chronology: W A Munford (ed) Annals of the Library Association 1877 to 1960 (LA, 1965). In the first edition of this book, I described the Annals as ' the bare bones of the LA's history ', but on reflection this is not altogether fair. Many of its entries are quite informative and in the section for the period 1877-1938 there are several characteristic comments by Dr Savage, who compiled it.

The best introductions to the LA's history are the article by Graham Jones in Landau's Encyclopaedia and W A Munford Penny rate (LA, 1951) chapter XV. There is a formal history of the LA, up to the 1920's, in John Minto A history of the public library movement (LA, 1932) chapters XII to XV and an informal review by Frank Pacy in Thornton's Selected readings chapter 40. On Carnegie and the LA see J G Ollé 'Andrew Carnegie: the unloved benefactor ' The library world LXX (826) April 1969 256.

On the history of the LA during the present century see W A Munford ' The Library Association in the twentieth century ' in D J Foskett and B I Palmer (eds) The Sayers memorial volume (LA, 1961), D D Haslam ' The Library Association ' in Robert F Vollans (ed) Libraries for the people: international studies in librarianship in honour of Lionel R McColvin (LA, 1968), Charles Nowell ' The LA in wartime ' Library Association record 47 (2) February 1945 24-30 and D D Haslam ' The fighting fifties ' Library Association record 62 (1) January 1960 2-10.

On the work done for the LA by some of its distinguished members see W A Munford *James Duff Brown* (LA, 1968), W G Fry and W A Munford *Louis Stanley Jast* (LA, 1966), Ernest A Savage *A librarian's memories* (Grafton, 1952) and *Libraries for the people,* in particular chapter 2, which pays tribute to the work of Lionel McColvin.

There is a lively description of the conference which brought the LA into being in B Gambee ' The great junket' *Journal of library history* II (1) January 1967 9-44. See also W A Munford ' Nicholson of the Bodleian' *Library review* XVIII (143) Autumn 1962 507-512.

There is no history of the AAL, but see the article by Graham Jones in Landau's *Encyclopaedia,* the jubilee symposium in the *Library assistant* 38 (5) September 1945, and the further symposium on the occasion of the diamond jubilee in the *Assistant librarian* 48 (4) April 1955. There is also a history of the AAL's journal: Stuart Brewer 'Assistant history' *Assistant librarian* 61 (8 9 11) August September and November 1968 176-179 208-211 244-249.

On the history of the other sections of the LA see F E Cook ' Lampadephoria: or the progress of the County Libraries Section', A C Townsend ' The University and Research Section 1928-1952 ' and W J Bishop ' The Medical Section ' in *Proceedings of the annual conference of the Library Association 1952,* Peggy Heeks ' Youth Libraries Group 1947-1968 ' *Library Association record* 70 (11) November 1968 283-284, and E Hargreaves ' RSIS 1950-1969 ' *The library world* LXXI (832) October 1969 105-108.

The Association of Special Libraries and Information Bureaux, which now has the registered title of Aslib, was founded in 1924 ' to facilitate the co-ordination and systematic use of sources of knowledge and information in all public affairs and in industry and commerce and in all the arts and sciences '. In its early years it was nearly extinguished by the depression, and its existence was again in peril at the beginning of the war. But the war gave it the opportunity to demonstrate its value to the nation, and since 1944 it has been aided by government grants. Post-war expansion in special librarianship has led to increased membership, a wider range of activities and the creation of subject groups.

On the early years see R S Hutton ' The origin and history of Aslib ' *Journal of documentation* 1 (1) June 1945 6-20 and E M R Ditmas ' Looking back on Aslib ' *Library review* XVIII winter 1961 268-274. On the general history see the article by Leslie Wilson in Landau's *Encyclopaedia*.

EDUCATION FOR LIBRARIANSHIP

In 1869, Edward Edwards wrote ' The day will come when in Britain we shall have courses of bibliography and of bibliothecal-economy for the training of librarians ' *(Free town libraries* 30). Unfortunately, we had examinations long before we had suitable courses.

When looking at the old LA syllabuses, examination papers and pass lists, it is easy to become satirical about the history of library education in Britain. But although there were errors and delays, it is to the credit of the association that many of its senior members worked willingly and hard examining, teaching and planning in the cause of professional education, among them Brown, Jast, Ogle, Ballinger, Savage, Baker and Sayers. Even Tedder, much criticised by Savage, was interested in the training of library assistants (see Thornton's *Selected readings* chapter 30). The first LA examinations were held in 1885. Summer schools were started in 1893, part time classes (in London) in 1898 and correspondence courses in 1904. The LA itself ran correspondence courses until 1930, when they were taken over by the AAL. For many years they were the only instruction available to most LA candidates.

The first school of librarianship was established at University College, London, with the help of the CUKT, in 1919. There were no more schools until 1946, in which year a new syllabus of examinations came into force, as a first step towards providing an examination system comparable to those of other professions. But even in the late 1950's, more than half of the candidates had received no full time professional education. This did not become common until the next revision of the LA syllabus came into force, in 1964.

' The history of library education in the United Kingdom ', said Sir Frank Francis, speaking at an international conference on library education in 1967, ' is interesting in itself from a sociological point of view, but it offers in my opinion regrettably little that is spectacular or indeed significant for the progress of library education anywhere else '. There are many librarians who would endorse this remark, but it is worth noting that American librarians, who have had the advantage of library schools, with their own syllabuses, for the greater part of a century, are as little satisfied with the present state of library education as we are. Robert B Downs has said, however, that ' This is a healthy state of affairs, for the field is never static and should be constantly reexamined and reevaluated '.

There is now a history of library education in the UK in Gerald Bramley *A history of library education* (Bingley, 1969) 11-71. It is impossible, however, to do justice to the complicated story of library education in this country in sixty pages and several important matters are disposed of far too rapidly. Nevertheless, this is a very readable history and it brings together, for the first time, a number of essential facts. See also the excellent paper by Sir Frank Francis, ' Education for librarianship in Great Britain ' in Larry Earl Bone (ed) *Library education: an international survey* (University of Illinois Graduate School of Library Science, 1968) 55-71 and ' Education for librarianship ' by Roy Stokes in Landau's *Encyclopaedia.*

CHAPTER SIXTEEN

LIBRARY HISTORY OF THE USA

I said earlier that the study of library history begins at home and commonly stays there. Few British librarians have taken much interest in American library history, which is a pity, for it is not only interesting in its own right but also because, since the end of the seventeenth century, it is linked with our own library history in many ways.

The library activities of Thomas Bray were divided between both countries. The early eighteenth century book clubs in England inspired the establishment of similar clubs in New England, but the American colonists then took the lead by founding larger book societies for the establishment of 'social libraries' (ie private subscription libraries).

The public library movement began in Britain and in the USA about the same time, although in different ways. The Library Association of the United Kingdom was founded one year after the American Library Association, and for several years the two associations shared the same journal. The work of Cutter, Dewey and Poole, in the respective fields of cataloguing, classification and periodical indexing, soon became as well-known in Britain as in the USA. The university libraries of the USA began late, but since the nineteenth century they have grown faster than British university libraries, with the exception of the copyright libraries of Oxford and Cambridge. According to Kruzas, there were about 400 company libraries in the USA by 1920, at which time there were hardly any in Britain.

The development of the Library of Congress as a national library during the present century has by no means been overlooked in this country. In fact, it has provided critics of the British Museum Library with some of their heaviest ammunition.

A very striking difference between library development in the two countries is to be found in the history of education in librarianship. Dewey started the first school of librarianship at

Columbia in 1887. There was no school in Britain until 1919 and this remained the only one until 1946.

Unfortunately, the study of American library history is in several ways even more difficult than the study of our own and for the same reason: the lack of authoritative general studies in many areas. According to Michael Harris, American librarians have shown little interest in the history of libraries and librarianship in the USA (*A guide to research in American library history* 9). But it would seem that interest is increasing. In 1947 the ALA American Library History Round Table was formed, mainly through the efforts of Louis Shores and Wayne Shirley. The Round Table organises occasional library history seminars and it has strong links with the quarterly *Journal of library history* (Florida State University Library School, Tallahassee), which began publication in January 1966.

British librarians investigating American library history for the first time will encounter some unfamiliar terms, *eg* association library, mercantile library, social library, school district library. For definition of these and other terms see the introduction to Thelma Eaton (*ed*) *Contributions to American library history* (Champaign, Illinois, Illini Bookstore, 1961).

There are two chronologies of American library history. Much the better of the two, although it is not indexed, is Elizabeth W Stone *Historical approach to American library development: a chronological chart* (University of Illinois Graduate School of Library Science Occasional papers no 83, May 1967), which is amply annotated and carefully documented. Josephine Metcalfe Smith *A chronology of librarianship* (Scarecrow Press, 1968) is far less informative and poorly documented.

There is no large-scale general library history of the USA, although according to a note in the *Journal of library history* (October 1968) such a work is now being written by Jesse Shera. However, a very useful introduction is provided in the historical chapters of Jean Key Gates *Introduction to librarianship* (McGraw-Hill, 1968). See also Elmer D Johnson *A history of libraries in the western world* (Scarecrow Press, 1965) chapters 15-21.

There are two collections of miscellaneous essays on American library history. Thelma Eaton (*ed*) *Contributions to American library history* brings together some of the useful articles published during the last quarter of the nineteenth century and the beginning of this century. John David Marshall *An American library history reader* (Shoe String Press, 1961) is a collection of original papers.

The finest works on American library history are the regional histories of Shera and Ditzion. Jesse H Shera *Foundations of the public library: the origins of the public library movement in New England 1629-1855* (University of Chicago Press, 1949; reprinted Shoe String Press, 1965) ranks high in the library literature of the world. It is one of the few works on library history which can be commended both for its scholarship and for its literary merit. Shera's book is complemented by Sidney Ditzion *Arsenals of a democratic culture* (ALA, 1947), a social history of the public library movement in New England and the middle states from 1850 to 1900. Reviewing this book in the *Journal of documentation* (March 1948 272-273), Ernest Savage said ' Had there been a book written in this country from the same standpoint, Dr Trevelyan's *Social history* would not be without reference to our own movement '.

Because of his work in Maryland and other colonies, Dr Thomas Bray occupies an important place in American library history which has been generously acknowledged. There are several published and unpublished studies of the Bray libraries in America. The more accessible references are Bernard C Steiner ' Rev Thomas Bray and his American libraries ', reprinted in *Contributions to American library history,* and W D Houlette ' Parish libraries and the work of the Rev Thomas Bray ' *Library quarterly* 4 (4) October 1934 588-609.

Dr Louis Shores, who has done much to stimulate interest in library history in America, is the author of *Origins of the American college library* 1638-1800 (Barnes & Noble, 1935; reprinted Shoe String Press, 1966). This is a pioneer history of the early development of academic libraries in the USA; unfortunately it has been reprinted without having been revised.

There is no comprehensive history of the public library movement in America. C Seymour Thompson *Evolution of the
American public library 1653-1876* (Scarecrow Press, 1952) is a
readable work on the forerunners of the modern public library
and its early history, but it suffers in comparison with the histories
of Shera and Ditzion, which cover part of the same ground. Robert
E Lee *Continuing education for adults through the American
public library 1833-1964* (ALA, 1966) is a study of the American
public library's role in adult education, an interesting theme but
one which requires more research to do it justice. George S Bobinski *Carnegie libraries: their history and impact on American
public library development* (ALA, 1969) should be of interest to
British librarians more than any other work on American library
history. The first and obvious reason is that it deals with an
important and fascinating aspect of American library history
which has its counterpart in British library history. The second
reason is that Dr Bobinski has made excellent use of the Carnegie
archives, and his book is admirably planned and lucidly written.
It does not tell the whole story, of course, as there is a good deal
of material on Carnegie's benefactions in local archives. In
America, as in the UK, there is still much work to do on the history
of individual public libraries. Some of the work which has already
been done in America on the history of individual public libraries
is of singular interest, however, as it is on a much larger scale, and
sometimes of a much higher standard than the histories of individual public libraries which have been published in this country.
Good examples are Gwladys Spencer *The Chicago Public Library*
(University of Chicago Press, 1943), Walter Muir Whitehill *Boston Public Library: a centennial history* (Harvard University
Press, 1956) and Frank B Woodford *Parnassus on Main Street: a
history of the Detroit Public Library* (Wayne State University
Press, 1965).

According to Thelma Eaton, Herbert Putnam, the distinguished
Librarian of Congress 1899-1939, planned a series of authoritative
studies in American library history. The plan never matured,
however, and the only volume published, out of the several which
were written, was W Dawson Johnston *History of the Library of*

Congress 1800-1864 (Library of Congress, 1904). The most useful history of the L of C is David Mearns *The story up to now*, originally published as part of the *Annual report of the Librarian of Congress for the fiscal year ending June 30 1946* (Library of Congress, 1947). This has also been published separately. See also Arundell Esdaile and F J Hill *National libraries of the world* (LA, 1957) chapter XXII.

A T Kruzas *Business and industrial libraries in the United States 1820-1940* (Special Libraries Association, 1965) is a worthy attempt to trace the history of commercial and industrial libraries (company libraries). Its limitations are not altogether the fault of the author. His book shows how difficult it is to investigate special library history through published sources of information.

There is no recent history of the American Library Association, but the story is outlined in the *Encyclopedia of library and information science* and in Landau's *Encyclopaedia*. There is a full account of the first organised meeting of librarians in the USA in G B Utley *The librarians' conference of 1853* (ALA, 1951).

There is a fairly large literature on the history of education for librarianship in the USA. An excellent introduction to this topic is Robert B Downs ' Education for librarianship in the United States and Canada ' in Larry Earl Bone *(ed) Library education : an international survey* (University of Illinois Graduate School of Library Science, 1968) 1-20, which provides further references.

One area of American library history is fairly well covered. Over seventy librarians are included in the *Dictionary of American biography*. They may be readily identified by consulting the index of occupations. A few American librarians are included in Thornton's *Selected readings in the history of librarianship*, namely, Cutter, Green, Billings, Dewey, Dana, Putnam and Bishop.

In the 1920's the ALA inaugurated a useful series of brief biographies called 'American library pioneers'. This series includes the following titles: H M Lyndenberg *John Shaw Billings* (1924), R K Shaw *Samuel Swett Green* (1926), W P Cutter *Charles Amni Cutter* (1931), Linda A Eastman *William Howard Brett* (1940), Chalmers Hadley *John Cotton Dana* (1943), Fremont Rider *Melvil Dewey* (1944) and Joseph A Borome *Charles Coffin Jewett*

(1951). The series is augmented by a volume of short biographical studies: Emily Miller Danton (ed) *Pioneering leaders in librarianship first series* (ALA, 1953).

There are several good large scale biographies, among them William Landram Williamson *William Frederick Poole and the modern library movement* (Columbia University Press, 1963), Edward G Holley *Charles Evans: American bibliographer* (University of Illinois Press, 1963) and Maurice F Tauber *Louis Round Wilson* (Columbia University Press, 1967).

Only in recent years has there been an appreciable number of theses on British library history. Theses on American library history have been written since the beginning of the century. Michael H Harris *A guide to research in American library history* (Scarecrow Press, 1968) is an admirable classified and annotated bibliography of masters' theses and doctoral dissertations accepted over the period 1908-1965. The introductory chapters on the present state of American library history are well worth reading. One of the several interesting observations made by Dr Harris is that ' One need only look at the best monographic studies on American library history to see that most of them were originally written as theses or dissertations in library schools or history departments '. For the time being this is not true of library history studies in the UK.

The references to American library history in this chapter have been deliberately restricted to a few titles. Further references will be found in the American chapters of Johnson's *A history of libraries in the western world* and in Michael H Harris ' Library history: a critical essay on the in-print literature ' *Journal of library history* II (2) April 1967 117-125.

By the end of 1969, only two volumes of the *Encyclopedia of library and information science* had been published, but it is evident that, in due course, this will be a ready source of information on many aspects of American library history.

The best sources of information on new writings on American library history are the review sections of the *Journal of library history* and the *Library quarterly*. The *Library quarterly*, which was founded in 1931, has published many valuable articles on American, British and European library history.

Among the several works relating to American library history which have been reprinted in recent years, one is of particular interest. It has been said that modern librarianship began in America in 1876. In that remarkable year, the ALA and the *Library journal* were founded, the first edition of the *Decimal classification* was published and the US Bureau of Education issued its famous report *Public libraries in the United States of America*. This was reprinted in 1965 by the University of Illinois Graduate School of Library Science.

INDEX

Royal Society of London Library 105-106

Ruddiman, Thomas 88

Savage, Ernest A 9, 18, 116

Science Museum Library 90-91

Scotland, general library history 28
  parochial libraries 49-50
  subscription libraries 52
  circulating libraries 57
  mechanics' institutes 62-63
  early town libraries 69
  itinerating libraries 70-71
  National Library of Scotland 88, 101-102

Select Committee on Public Libraries
  see Ewart report

Shackleton report 98

Sloane Collection 84, 111, 113

Sloane, Sir Hans 111, 113

Smith, W H & Son, circulating libraries of 59-61

Smith, William Henry 59, 61

Society for promoting Christian Knowledge 45, 48

Special libraries 105-108

Subscription libraries 31-32, 51-56

Tedder, Henry 114-115

Terminology 11

Times Book Club 60

Town libraries 67-69

Trinity College Library, Dublin 98, 102

Trustees for Erecting Parochial Libraries 45, 47-48

Twopenny libraries 60-61

University Grants Committee 34, 99

University libraries 93-100

USA, general library history 122-123
  Library of Congress 122, 125-126
  education for librarianship 122-123, 126
  American Library History Round Table 123
  public libraries 124-125
  parochial libraries 124
  college libraries 124
  company libraries 126
  American Library Association 126
  biographical literature 126-127
  theses on library history 127

Victoria and Albert Museum Library 90

Village libraries, of Yorkshire 64-65
  of Scotland 70-71

Wanley, Humfrey 110, 112

Wright, Sir Charles Hagberg 54, 56

Yorkshire Union of Mechanics' Institutes 64-65